Meal Prep for Weight Loss

2 Books in 1

MEDITERRANEAN DIET COOKBOOK

&

MEDITERRANEAN DIET AIR FRYER COOKBOOK

© **Copyright 2020 - All rights reserved.**

The content contained within this book may not be reproduced, duplicated or transmitted without direct written permission from the author or the publisher.

Under no circumstances will any blame or legal responsibility be held against the publisher, or author, for any damages, reparation, or monetary loss due to the information contained within this book. Either directly or indirectly.

Legal Notice:

This book is copyright protected. This book is only for personal use. You cannot amend, distribute, sell, use, quote or paraphrase any part, or the content within this book, without the consent of the author or publisher.

Disclaimer Notice:

Please note the information contained within this document is for educational and entertainment purposes only. All effort has been executed to present accurate, up to date, and reliable, complete information. No warranties of any kind are declared or implied. Readers acknowledge that the author is not engaging in the rendering of legal, financial, medical or professional advice. The content within this book has been derived from various sources. Please consult a licensed professional before attempting any techniques outlined in this book.

By reading this document, the reader agrees that under no circumstances is the author responsible for any losses, direct or indirect, which are incurred as a result of the use of information contained within this document, including, but not limited to, — errors, omissions, or inaccuracies.

Mediterranean Diet Cookbook

Delicious, Easy & Healthy Mediterranean Diet Recipes for Everyday Meals to Weight Loss, Heal Your Body and Live a Healthy Lifestyle

Table of Contents

Chapter 1: A General Overview of The Mediterranean Diet..........................13

Introduction to The Mediterranean Diet
What is The Mediterranean Diet?
Components of The Mediterranean Diet

Chapter 2: Advantages and Benefits of the Mediterranean Diet..........................33

The Main Benefits of The Mediterranean Diet
How the Mediterranean Diet Can Help You
Risks and Potential Obstacles
Myths and Facts about The Mediterranean Diet
How to Make Changes
Quick Start of The Mediterranean Diet

Chapter 3: Example of A Balanced Meal Plan and Useful Tips That Will Help You Every Day..........................48

4-Week Mediterranean Diet Meal Plan
7-Days Mediterranean Diet Meal Plan

Chapter 4: Mediterranean Diet Breakfast Recipes..59

Mediterranean Breakfast Board

Egg Baked

Quinoa Breakfast Chili

Savory Steel Cut Oatmeal

Hummus and Vegetables Breakfast Bowl

Banana Mocha Overnight Oats

Avocado with Ketogenic Baked Eggs and Muddles Breakfast Jar

Chapter 5: Mediterranean Diet Lunch Recipes..81

Mediterranean Chicken Tacos

Mediterranean Quinoa Bowls with Roasted Red Poivrade

Greek Lemon Soup

Greek Fetus Salad

Harissa Salad

Greek Quinoa Bowls

Faroe Second with Ronnie Grease Chicken and Oven Fries

Wild Alaskan Salmon and Smoked Cucumber Cereal Bowls

Stuffed Brinjal

Greek Turkey Burger with Tzatziki Sauce

Eggplant Pizza

Greek Lemon Chicken with Tzatziki Soak

Salmon Bowl Faro, Black Beans and Tahini Dressing

Toasted Zaatar Pita Bread with Mezze Plater

Pesto Quinoa Bowls with Roasted Vegetables and Labneh

Mediterranean Couscous with Tuna and Pepperoncini

Herbs Flatbread

Mini Chicken Shawarma

Greek Chicken and Rice Skillet

Grilled Lemon-Herb Chicken and Avocado Salad

Harissa Kabuli Gram Stew with Eggplant

Salad with Grilled Halloumi and Herbs

Chapter 6: Mediterranean Diet Snack Recipes.....................................139

Blueberry Coconut Energy Bits

Mediterranean-Style Dip with Roasted Squash

Spring Peas + Fava Bean Guacamole with Root Chips.

Beet Chips

Greek Fried Zucchini

Greek Spinach Artichoke Dip

7-Ingredient Quinoa Granola

Mediterranean Roasted Gram

Smoked Eggplant Dip: Baba Ganesh

Crock Pot Chunky Monkey Paleo Trail Mix

Greek Guacamole

Roasted Veggie Chips

Homemade Taj Tiki-Style Sauce

Greek Hummus Pita Cutting

Rainbow Heirloom Tomato Bruschetta

Chapter 7: Mediterranean Diet Dinner Recipes..177

One-Pot Greek Chicken and Lemon Rice

Pan Mediterranean Cod

Mediterranean Couscous with Chicken Souvlaki Kebab

Garlic Swiss Chard & Chickpea Shed Swiss Chard

Spinach Feta Grilled Cheese

Mediterranean Chicken and Barley Salad

Chestnut-Henna Crusted Salmon

Sun-Dried Tomato and Feta Seth Couscous

Quinoa Tabbouleh

Vegetable Soup

Crotch Pot Chicken Thighs with Artichokes and Sun-Dried Tomatoes

Roasted Herbs Salmon

Greek Quesadillas

Chicken Piccata

Sweet Potato Noodles

Mediterranean Baked Sadist Potato Sweet Potatoes

Shrimp Noodles

Pineapple Chalk Seth Jerk Shrimp

Mediterranean Grilled Balsamic Chicken

Cheuk and Vegetable Coconut Curry

Bowl with Shirak + Winter Greens

Zucchini Lasagna Rolls

Vegan Smoky Moussaka

Salmon Souvlaki Bowls

Mediterranean Potato Hash with Asparagus, Chickpeas, and Illegal Eggs

Mediterranean Nachos

Avocado Tomato Gouda Soda Pizza

Conclusion..253

Chapter 1: A General Overview of The Mediterranean Diet

Congratulations on purchasing *Meal Prep for Weight Loss* and thank you for doing so.

Introduction to The Mediterranean Diet

It is commonly accepted that parents in Mediterranean countries live and suffer longer. Still, most Americans suffer from cancer and cardiovascular diseases. The not-so-surprising secret is a vibrant lifestyle, weight control, and a diet low in meat, sugar, and saturated fat and high production, nuts, and other healthy foods. The Mediterranean diet can provide many health benefits, including weight loss, heart and brain health, cancer prevention, and diabetes prevention and control. By following the Mediterranean diet, you will reduce that weight while avoiding chronic disease.

There is no "one" Mediterranean diet. Greeks eat differently from Greeks, Italians, and Greeks who eat differently. But they share many similar principles.

Working with the Harvard School of Public Health in Boston, a nonprofit food thinks factory in Boston has developed a consumer-friendly Mediterranean diet pyramid that gives directions on how to fill your plate - and perhaps wineglass - Mediterranean way.

Because it is often a pattern of eating - not a structured diet - you are at your task as to what percentage of calories you consume to lose or maintain your weight, which you will do to stay active and the way you do Shape your Mediterranean menu. The Mediterranean Diet Pyramid should help you get started. The pyramid emphasizes eating fruits, vegetables, whole grains, beans, nuts, legumes, olive oil, and tasty herbs and spices, instead of fish and seafood at least a few times a week; And when saving sweets and meat for special occasions, consider chicken, eggs, cheese, and yogurt carefully. Top it off with a splash of alcohol (if you want to); remember to stay physically active, and you're set.

While never required, a glass each day for women and twice each day for men is fine if your doctor says so. The wine has gained a lift because it contains resveratrol, a compound that takes years to live - but you'll probably need to drink hundreds or thousands of glasses to urge enough resveratrol to make a difference.

The cost of the Mediterranean diet, like most aspects of the diet, depends on how you shape it; While some ingredients (nuts, olive oil, fish and especially fresh produce) are often expensive, you'll find ways to keep the tabs reasonable - especially if you replace red meats and meals with plant-based home cooking. Are, so some research suggests. Your shopping choice also matters. Can't spring for a $ 50 wine bottle? Grab one for $ 15 instead. And instead of the $ 3-a-piece artichoke, whatever is on sale that day, snag. Mediterranean diet can help you reduce it. While some people fear that eating a diet like the Mediterranean diet that is relatively rich in fat (think vegetable oil, olives, avocados, and some cheese) will keep them fat, more and more research suggests the second is true. Of course, it depends on what aspects you adopt and how your current diet compares. If, as an example, you create a "calorie deficit" in your plan - by eating fewer calories than your daily recommended maximum or burning extra by exercising - you should shed a few pounds. How soon and whether you want to maintain them is up to you.

Here's a look at a couple of studies addressing weight loss on the Mediterranean diet:

A 2018 study published in Nutrition and Diabetes analyzed the dietary patterns of 32,119 Italian participants over the course of 12 years. Researchers concluded that following the Mediterranean diet is related to lower levels of weight gain and fewer increases in waist circumference. But they also report that research has limitations that require more intervention studies to verify their findings.

In 2019, The Lancet Diabetes and Endocrinology Journal republished an updated analysis of knowledge from predetermined - 5,859 adults (including 1,588 participants who dropped out of the five-year trial when the study was withdrawn and republished in 2017) in type 2 diabetes. Or at risk for the disorder. Those who were assigned either a Mediterranean diet supplemented with vegetable oil, a diet supplemented with nuts, or an effective diet. Although the group with vegetable oil did not experience a statistically different result, those who followed the Mediterranean diet with nuts noticed a difference in waistline over a period of five years.

A 2010 study in diabetes, obesity, and metabolism gave 259 overweight, diabetic patients at least one of three diets: a low-carb Mediterranean diet, a standard Mediterranean diet, or a diet-backed recommendation from the American Diabetes Association. All groups were asked to exercise a minimum of 30 to 45 minutes 3 times per week. After one year, all groups lost their weight; The general group lost a mean of about 16 pounds, while the ADA group lost 17 pounds, and therefore the low-carb group lost 22 pounds.

A 2008 analysis of 21 studies within the Obesity Review-journal concluded that the jury maintains that following the Mediterranean diet will reduce weight or the likelihood of being overweight or obese.

Because Mediterranean diets do not ban whole food groups, you should not have trouble complying with it in the future.

The Mediterranean diet is often convenient. Once you want to cook, there is a recipe and complimentary wine that will take you across the Atlantic. Consumer-friendly tips from Old ways will make meal planning and prepping easier. And you will dine outside if you share the oddity to bring someone along.

Old ways offer several Mediterranean dishes, including a food specialty guide that each cost $ 2 or less. Otherwise, an easy Google search will allow many healthy Mediterranean food ideas to occur. Want more inspiration? Old ways to recommend a "4-week Mediterranean diet menu plan."

If you dine following a Mediterranean diet, share the intimacy of the food by ordering an entry for 2 of you. And be sure to start out with a house salad or urge extra veggies to fill up a la carte.

You can save time on the Mediterranean diet by cooking ahead of time and storing food; Otherwise, you will have to hire someone to plan, buy and prepare your meal, if some time is worth more than your wallet.

You will find lots of free Mediterranean dietary resources on the Old ways website, including an easy food pyramid; A printable grocery list; Gender- and age-specific recommendations for making Mediterranean switches; A quick read "starter" brochure;

A recipe newspaper; And even defining a literal Mediterranean staple, from Bruschetta to Tapenade.

Hunger should not be a drag on this diet; Filling fiber and healthy fats, and you are eating many fiber-packed products and whole grains, and cooking with saturated fats like vegetable oils. Nutritionists emphasize the importance of satiety and a feeling satisfied with what you've got.

What is The Mediterranean Diet?

The Mediterranean diet may have been a diet invented within us within the 1980s and inspired by the eating habits of Italy and Greece within the 1960s. The main aspects of this diet include vegetable oils, legumes, unrefined grains, fruits and vegetables, high consumption of fish, moderate consumption of dairy products (mostly in the form of cheese and yogurt), moderate alcohol consumption, and low proportionally high Consumption included.

Consumption of non-fish meat products: Vegetable oil has been studied as a potential health factor to reduce all possible mortality and, therefore, the risk of chronic diseases.

Mediterranean diet correlates with all-mortality remission in observational studies. There is some evidence that a Mediterranean diet reduces heart conditions and the risk of early death, although a 2019 review determined that the evidence was inferior and uncertain. The American Heart Association and the American Diabetes Association recommend the Mediterranean diet as a healthy dietary pattern that will reduce the risk of heart diseases and diabetes 2, respectively. Mediterranean diet can help in weight loss in obese people. The Mediterranean diet is one of three healthy diets recommended within the 2015–2020 US dietary guidelines, including the DASH diet or the vegetarian diet.

The Mediterranean Diet as a nutritional recommendation differs from the cultural practices that UNESCO listed in 2010 in the representative list of the Intangible Cultural Heritage of Humanity under the heading "Mediterranean Diet": "Skills, knowledge, rituals, symbols, and traditions." A group. Fertilizers, harvesting, fishing, farming, preservation, processing, cooking, and especially concerning food sharing and consumption Not as a specific set of substances. Its sponsors include Italy, Spain, Portugal, Morocco, Greece, Cyprus, and Croatia.

The Mediterranean diet is included among dietary patterns that will reduce the risk of heart diseases. 2013 K Kuchen's review found limited evidence that the Mediterranean diet favors cardiovascular risk factors favorably. In the Mediterranean with a control diet, a 2013 meta-analysis comparing vegetarian, vegan, low glycemic index, low carbohydrate, high fiber, and high protein diets. The research concluded that Mediterranean, low carbohydrate, low glycemic index, and high-protein diet are associated with increased risk of disorder and diabetes. Are effective in improving markers, while limited evidence for glycemic control and the effect of vegetarian diets on lipid levels Were related to weight loss. However, early 2016 reviews are more cautious: concern has been expressed about the standard of previous systematic reviews examining the effects of the Mediterranean diet on cardiovascular risk factors, further standardized research has been found to be necessary, and therefore potential prevention. Evidence for the vascular disease was "limited and highly variable" by the Mediterranean diet. In 2016–17, the review reached similar conclusions about the power of a Mediterranean diet to increase cardiovascular risk factors, such as reducing the risk for high blood pressure and other cardiovascular diseases.

The Mediterranean diet is low in saturated fat with monounsaturated fat and high amounts of dietary fiber. One possible factor is the potential health effects of vegetable oil within the Mediterranean diet. Vegetable oil contains monounsaturated fat, most notably monounsaturated fatty acids, which are under clinical research for its potential health benefits. Nutrition Food Safety Authority Panel on dietary products, approved health claims on nutrition and allergy vegetable oil, to cover by its polyphenols against oxidation of blood lipids and to replace saturated fats in normal blood LDL-cholesterol levels for contributing to sustaining. Diet with monounsaturated fatty acids (Commission Regulation (EU) 432/2012 on 16 May 2012). A 2014 meta-analysis concluded that higher consumption of vegetable oil correlated with a lower risk of all-cause mortality, stroke, and cardiovascular events, while monounsaturated fatty acids of mixed animal and plant origin showed no significant effect.

The American Heart Association discussed the Mediterranean diet as a healthy dietary pattern, which would reduce the risk of heart diseases.

Diabetes

In 2014, two meta-analyses found that the Mediterranean diet was related to a lower risk of type 2 diabetes, with findings almost like the 2017 review. The American Diabetes Association and the 2019 review indicated that the Mediterranean diet might be a healthy dietary pattern that will reduce the risk of diabetes.

Cancer

A meta-analysis in 2008 found that strictly following the Mediterranean diet reduced the risk of dying from cancer by 6%. Another 2014 review found that following a Mediterranean diet was related to a lower risk of death from cancer. The 2017 review noted a decrease in cancer rates, although the evidence was weak.

Reducing Obesity

A 2019 review in the Mediterranean diet was discussed as a dietary pattern that would help obese people reduce the number and improve the nutritional quality of food intake, possibly with the overall effect of losing weight.

Cognitive Ability

A 2016 systematic review found a relationship between greater adherence to the Mediterranean diet and improved cognitive performance; It is not clear whether the connection is the cause.

According to a 2013 systematic review, greater adherence to a Mediterranean diet is associated with a lower risk of Alzheimer's disease and slower cognitive decline. A more systematic review of 2013 arrived at similar conclusions and found a negative association with the risk of progression from mild cognitive impairment for Alzheimer's but acknowledged that only a small number of studies had been conducted on this topic.

The major clinical depression is the association between adherence to the Mediterranean diet and lower risk of depression. The studies on which these correlations are built are observable and do not prove cause and effect.

Gluten

Mediterranean diet usually includes gluten-containing products such as pasta and bread; the increased use of the diet may have contributed to the increasing rate of gluten-related disorders.

Aging There Is some evidence that greater adherence to the Mediterranean diet is associated with longer telomeres. The concept of the Mediterranean diet was developed to reflect "typical dining patterns of Crete, much of the remainder of Greece, and Italy within the 1960s". Although it was first promoted in 1975 by American biologist Ansell Keys and chemist Margaret Keys (his wife and colleague), the Mediterranean diet was not widely recognized until the 1990s. This indicates that the Mediterranean diet originated from the results of epidemiological studies in Naples and Madrid, confirmed by studies from the first seven countries in 1970 and later by a book-length report in 1980.

The most understood version of the Mediterranean diet was introduced by Walter Willett and colleagues of the School of Public Health at Harvard University, among others, from the mid-1990s. The Mediterranean diet is predicated on a paradox: although people living in Mediterranean countries consume relatively high amounts of fat, they have far fewer disorders than those in countries like ours that have similar levels of fat consumption. It is needed. A parallel phenomenon is understood to be due to the French paradox. As of 2011, the Mediterranean diet was included by some authors as a reduced diet promoting weight loss. By 2018, the value of common Mediterranean diets for the harmonization of dietary choices and food products within the global economy was questioned, yet clinical research activity remained at a high level, with favorable results reported for various disease conditions, Such as metabolic syndrome.

Surprise! No Calorie Counting

You will not need a calculator for this hotel plan. Instead of adding numbers, you swap out bad fats for heart-healthy people. Choose vegetable oil instead of butter. Try fish or chicken instead of meat. Enjoy fresh fruit and skip sweet, fancy desserts.

Eat your delicious flavored beans and beans. Nuts are good, but being with a couple every day. You will have whole grain bread and wine but in moderate amounts.

The Food is Basically Fresh

You won't bump into a frozen food aisle or bump into a fast-food drive-through. The focus is on seasonal food made with simple, mouth-watering methods. Make a delicious salad with spinach, cucumbers, and tomatoes. Add classic Greek ingredients such as black Greek and feta cheese with a fast, light Greek salad recipe. You'll whip up a colorful, veggie-filled batch of grilled tomato gazpacho.

You can apply bread for whole bread made of whole grains. It has got more protein and minerals and is generally healthier than the white flour type. Try whole-grain ground bread dipped in vegetable oil, hummus or tahini (a protein-rich paste made from ground sesame).

Fat is Not Forbidden: You Just Got to Search for Right Types

You will find it in nuts, olives, and vegetable oil. These fats (saturated and not trans fats hidden in processed foods) add flavor and help fight diseases ranging from diabetes to cancer. Basic Basil Pesto can be delicious to get something in your diet.

The Menu is Large

It is quite simply Greek and Italian cuisine. Discover the cuisine of Spain, Turkey, Morocco, and other countries. Choose foods that stick with the basics: light on meat and whole-fat dairy, along with many fresh fruits and vegetables, olive oil, and whole grains. This Moroccan recipe with okra, chickpeas, and spices fits into the healthy Mediterranean profile.

Spices Delicious

Add bay leaf, cilantro, coriander, rosemary, garlic, pepper, cinnamon, and so much flavor that you will not get the saltshaker. Some also have health benefits. Coriander and rosemary, for example, are antioxidants and nutrients that fight disease. This recipe for Greek-style mushrooms uses cilantro and coriander and features a linear kick.

As it is small, easy to collect, Greek food is often called easy plates. For your own serve-it-cold casual meal, you will put out plates of cheese, olives, and nuts. Also, observe these dishes for basil quinoa with red bell peppers and eight layered Greek dips. Both contain heart-friendly ingredients, including vegetable oils, beans, whole grains, and spices.

You Can Have Wine

A glass with food is common in many Mediterranean countries, where food is usually leisurely and socially. Some studies suggest that for some people, up to at least one glass every day for women and two for men may also be good for your heart. Alcohol can also be healthier than white. Ask your doctor to find out if this is a good idea for you.

You Not feel hungry will, you will get a chance to eat rich flavored foods like roasted sweet potato, hummus, and even this lima bean spread. You digest them slowly so that you are feeling for a long time. Hungry when you can crave a bite of nuts, olives, or low-fat cheese when a craving strike. Feta and halloumi are lower in fat than cheddar but still rich and attractive.

You can reduce it, if you eat nuts, cheese, and oil, it can be a miracle to drop a few pounds. But those Mediterranean basics (and slow eating style) allow you to feel full and satisfied. Which helps you stick to the diet. Regular exercise is additionally an important part of the lifestyle.

Many thanks to your heart. During this diet, almost everything is sweet for your heart. Vegetable oils and nuts help reduce ´ 'bad" cholesterol. Fruits, vegetables, and beans help keep the arteries clean. The fish helps in reducing triglycerides and vital signs. Even a daily glass of wine can be good for your heart! If you've never been mad with fish, do a Mediterranean-inspired recipe for grilled whole trout with lemon-tarragon bean salad.

You Will Remain a Sharp Lounger

The same goodness that protects your heart is additionally good for your brain. You are not eating bad fats and processed foods, which can cause inflammation.

Instead, antioxidant-rich foods make this eating style a brain-friendly choice.

Interest within the Mediterranean diet began within the 1960s with the observation that coronary heart conditions led to fewer deaths in Mediterranean countries such as Greece and Italy than in the US and northern Europe. Subsequent studies found that the Mediterranean correlated with lower risk factors the dietary disorder.

The Mediterranean diet is one of the healthier eating plans recommended by the Dietary Guidelines to prevent Americans' health and chronic disease.

It is also recognized by the Planet Health Organization as a healthy and sustainable dietary pattern and as an intangible cultural asset by the United National Educational, Scientific, and Cultural Organization.

Components of The Mediterranean Diet

The Mediterranean diet can be a way to support the common cuisine of countries bordering the Mediterranean Sea. While there is no single definition of the Mediterranean diet, it is generally high in vegetables, fruits, whole grains, beans, walnuts and seeds, and vegetable oil.

The main components of the Mediterranean diet include:

Daily consumption of vegetables, fruits, whole grains, and healthy fats, weekly intake of fish, poultry, legumes, and eggs, moderate portions of dairy products. Limited intake of meat, other important elements of the Mediterranean diet are sharing food with family and friends, enjoying a glass of wine, and being physically active.

Plant-Based - Not Meat-Based

Mediterranean diets are the basis of vegetables, fruits, herbs, nuts, beans, and whole grains. Food is built around these plant-based foods. Moderate amounts of dairy, poultry, and eggs as seafood are also central to the Mediterranean diet. In contrast, meat is seldom eaten.

Healthy Fat

Healthy fat is a mainstay of the Mediterranean diet. They are eaten instead of less healthy fats, such as saturated and trans fats, which contribute to heart conditions.

Olive oil is the primary source of excess fat within the Mediterranean diet. Vegetable oil provides monounsaturated fats, which have been found to lower total cholesterol and LDL

(LDL or "bad") cholesterol levels. Nuts and seeds also contain monounsaturated fat.

Fish are also important within the Mediterranean diet. Fatty fish - such as mackerel, herring, sardines, albacore tuna, salmon, and lake trout - are rich in omega-3 fatty acids, a type of fat that will reduce inflammation within the body. Omega-3 fatty acids also help in reducing triglycerides, reducing blood coagulation, and reducing the risk of stroke and coronary failure.

What about Alcohol?

The Mediterranean diet usually allows alcohol to concentrate. Although alcohol has been related to a lower risk of heart conditions in some studies, it is not harmless in any way. Dietary guidelines for Americans caution against the idea of potential health benefits of drinking more often.

Are Mediterranean diets interested in eating Mediterranean food?

The following prompts will help you get started:

- Eat more fruits and vegetables. Aim for 7 to 10 servings of fruits and vegetables each day.

- Opt for whole grains. Switch to whole grain bread, cereal and pasta. Use with other whole grains, such as bulgur and farro.
- Use healthy fats. While cooking, try vegetable oil as a replacement for butter. Instead of applying butter or margarine to the bread, try dipping it in fragrant vegetable oil.
- Eat more seafood. Eat fish twice every week. Fresh or waterlogged tuna, salmon, trout, mackerel, and herring are healthy options. Grilled fish tastes good and requires very little cleaning. Avoid deep-fried fish.
- Reduce meat: Substances, poultry, or legumes for meat. If you eat meat, confirm it to be lean and keep the portion small.
- Enjoy some dairy. Consume low-fat Greek or plain yogurt and small amounts of cheese.
- Spice it up. Herbs and spices enhance the taste and reduce the need for salt.

Chapter 2: Advantages and Benefits of the Mediterranean Diet

The Main Benefits of The Mediterranean Diet

1. Preserve Memory and Prevent Cognitive Decline

Filled with healthy fats for the brain, the Mediterranean diet is often good for increasing brain power and preventing dementia and cognitive decline. In one study, researchers found that major adherence to the Mediterranean diet was related to a 40 percent lower risk for cognitive impairment.

2. Reduce Your Risk for a Heart Condition

Studies show that following a Mediterranean diet can reduce your risk for the disorder, including coronary heart conditions, myocardial infarction (heart attack) and stroke.

This is thanks to the positive effects of the Mediterranean diet on cardiovascular risk factors, including high-risk signals, triglycerides, and cholesterol.

3. Strengthen Bones

One study suggests that some compounds in vegetable oil may help maintain bone density by increasing the proliferation and maturation of bone cells. Another study found that dietary patterns related to the Mediterranean diet may help prevent osteoporosis.

4. Manage Diabetes and Control Blood Sugar

The Mediterranean diet has been shown to have beneficial effects on diabetes. It will be designed to prevent type 2 diabetes and may help improve blood sugar control and cardiovascular risk in those who have already received it.

When the Mediterranean diet was compared to the diet, people with type 2 diabetes followed the Mediterranean diet; Fewer people needed treatment, and they experienced greater weight loss and better blood sugar control.

5. Fight Depression

People following the Mediterranean diet can also be protected from depression. A 2013 study found that people who followed the Mediterranean diet the most had a 98.6 percent lower risk of developing depression than people who had the smallest amount of it.

6. Avoid Cancer

High adherence to the Mediterranean diet can help prevent cancer. A scientific review of the studies found that overall, people who follow the diet have a 13 percent lower than the highest cancer mortality rate among those who follow the smallest amount. Carcinoma, colorectal cancer, gastric cancer, prostatic include. Adenocarcinoma, liver cancer, and head and neck cancer.

How The Mediterranean Diet Can Help You

To practice this, on a Mediterranean diet, you should eat fruits, vegetables, and healthy fats like vegetable oil several times per day; Legumes and unrefined whole grains at least once a day; And fish, nuts, and seeds several times per week. Saturated fats and refined sugars should be limited to special occasions only.

1. It Is Good for Your Heart

"This is probably the most important known benefit," Moore says. "Mediterranean diet has been shown to reduce the risk of heart condition, stroke, and early death, all related to improved heart health." This is because this diet is high in heart-healthy omega-3s as an antioxidant from c-food, nuts, and vegetable oils as well as all those fruits and vegetables.

2. It Increases Brain Health

All those healthy fats are also good for your brain. A study with 1,864 participants found that those following a Mediterranean diet were less likely to experience Alzheimer's urge or experience other types of cognitive decline in adulthood. In fact, there is an immediate correlation between fish consumption and the low risk of Alzheimer's.

3. It can help with depression and anxiety

Due to psychiatrist and Well + Good Wellness counselor Drew Ramsey, MD is a vegetable and healthy fat-rich diet that makes it a part of their treatment for patients with depression, anxiety, or other psychiatric conditions: bananas, spinach, and eggs are great in your gut. Bacteria have been shown to spice up, and serially, your mood. One study found that when older adults followed the

Mediterranean diet, they were less likely to experience depression.

4. It can help stabilize blood sugar

Unlike other popular eating plans, the Mediterranean diet is big on whole grains and other healthy carbs - and comes with huge benefits. Says Beckman, "Complex whole-grain carbohydrates instead of refined grains, such as buckwheat, wheat berries, and quinoa, help maintain your blood sugar levels as well as help with all your energy. "

5. It is associated with reducing the risk of cancer

When researchers examined a combined 27 studies - considering more than 2 million people - they found that the Med diet is that eating plans are associated with a lower risk of cancer ethics, especially carcinoma, carcinoma, and gastric cancer. Is connected

6. It promotes healthy weight management

"Because of all the fiber, the Mediterranean diet is useful in managing fullness," Moore says. "You feel more satisfied with foods high in fiber, which helps in healthy weight loss and metabolism." The key: replacing simple carbohydrates with fibrous fruits, vegetables, legumes, and beans.

7. It is a special benefit for post-menopausal women

Get this: Mediterranean diet has also been linked to positive effects of bone and muscle in post-menopausal women. This was little study, so more research is needed, but it is promising because previous studies have found that menopause can reduce the bone and muscle of women.

8. It is good for your stomach

One study has found that people who follow a Mediterranean diet have a better population of excellent bacteria in their microbiome than those who eat a standard Western diet. Researchers noted an increase in eating plant-based foods such as vegetables, fruits, and legumes, which put the great bacteria above 7 percent - not too shabby.

9. It is associated with prolonged stay

As if all the above benefits are not enough, it is also associated with living an extended life- mainly due to the above-mentioned better heart health. There is a reason why many of these "blue areas" are within the Mediterranean!

Risks and Potential Obstacles

Beckerman says, "You know, I don't think there's a warning for a Mediterranean diet. "Moore agrees but says people should be cautious of the new dietary mercury as they are increasing their seafood consumption. He focuses on isolating seafood sources and on shrimp, tuna, salmon, and catfish, such as swordfish and mackerel. Offers advice to choose low-mercury choices.

When you consider diet, your mind might include pizza and pasta, or lobe chops from Greece to Italy. These dishes do not fit into healthy diet plans advertised as "Mediterranean." A true Mediterranean diet is the region's traditional fruits, vegetables, beans, nuts, seafood, olive oil, and dairy - maybe a glass, or provided with two wines. Therefore, residents of Crete, Greece, and Southern Italy ate Circa in 1960, when their chronic disease rates around the world were found in Rock Bottom. Even though It was not only limited medical services, his anticipation was too far between, and are key elements of a true Mediterranean diet being nearly fresh, nutritious food, daily physical activity and diet pyramid Mediterranean to share food with others. Together, they will have a profound effect on your mood and psychological state and will foster a deep appreciation for the pleasure of eating healthy and delicious foods.

Of course, making changes to your diet is never easy, especially if you are trying to do away with the convenience of processed and takeout foods. But the Mediterranean diet is often cheaper and satisfying to eat and healthier. Making the switch from pepperoni and pasta to fish and avocado may take some effort, but you'll soon be on your way to a healthier and longer life.

Health Benefits of the Mediterranean Diet. A traditional Mediterranean diet consisting of many fresh fruits and vegetables, nuts, fish, and olive oil - combined with physical activity - can reduce the risk of great mental and physical health problems by you:

Heart condition and stroke. To stop Following a Mediterranean diet limits your intake of refined bread, processed foods, and meat, and encourages drinking instead of hard liquor - all factors that will help prevent heart conditions and strokes.

Keep you tight If you are an older adult, the nutrients obtained with the Mediterranean diet can reduce your risk of developing muscle weakness and other symptoms of waste by about 70 percent.

Reducing the risk of Alzheimer's: Research suggests that Mediterranean diets can improve cholesterol, blood sugar levels, and overall vessel health, which can progressively reduce the risk of Alzheimer's disease or dementia.

Reduced risk of Parkinson's disease: High levels of antioxidants within the Mediterranean diet can prevent cells from undergoing a deleterious process called oxidative stress, reducing the risk of Parkinson's disease by half.

Increasing Longevity. By reducing your risk of developing heart conditions or cancer with a Mediterranean diet, you are reducing your risk of death by 20% at any age.

Prevention from type 2 diabetes The Mediterranean diet is rich in fiber that digests slowly, prevents a massive drop in blood sugar, and can help you maintain a healthy weight.

Myths and Facts about The Mediterranean Diet

Following the Mediterranean diet has many benefits, but there are still many misconceptions about how to live a healthy, long-lived lifestyle to capitalize on the lifestyle. Later there are some myths and facts about the Mediterranean diet.

Myth 1: This method costs tons to eat.

Fact: If you are making a meal out of beans or lentils as your main source of protein, and are mostly studded with plants and whole grains, the Mediterranean diet is more expensive than serving packaged or processed foods. Is.

Myth 2: If one glass of wine is sweet for your heart, then three glasses are three times healthy.

Fact: A moderate amount of wine (one drink each day for women and two for men) certainly has unique health benefits for your heart, but drinking in excess will have a second effect. Anything quite two glasses of wine can be bad for your heart.

Myth 3: Eating large bowls of pasta and bread is the Mediterranean way

Usually, the Mediterranean does not eat a huge plate of pasta the way Americans do. Instead, pasta is typically a funeral with some 1/2-cup to 1-cup serving sizes. The remainder of their plate consists of salads, vegetables, fish, or a small portion of organic, grass-fed meat and perhaps a piece of bread.

Myth 4: The Mediterranean diet is only about food.

Fact: Food can be a big part of the diet, yes, but do not ignore the opposite ways to live a Mediterranean life. Once they sit for a meal, they do not sit in front of a TV or dine in a hurry; They sit with others for a relaxed, relaxed meal, which can be as important to your health as it is on your plate. The Mediterranean also enjoys many physical activities.

How to Make Changes

If you are feeling mad at yourself by thinking about adjusting, you're eating habits to the Mediterranean diet, here are some tips you urge to start:

Eat many vegetables. Try an easy plate of chopped tomatoes dripped with vegetable oil and crumbled cheese or load your thin crust pizza with chili and mushrooms instead of sausage and pepperoni. Instead, salads, soups, and crudité platters are also great for loading on vegetables.

Always have breakfast Fruits, whole grains, and other fiber-rich foods are excellent thanks to the start of your day, keeping you pleasantly plentiful for hours.

Eat seafood twice every week. Fishes such as tuna, salmon, herring, sablefish (black cod), and sardines are rich in omega-3 fatty acids, and shellfish such as muscles, oysters, and clams have similar benefits for brain and heart health.

Cook a vegetarian meal one night every week. If this is useful, you will hope for a trend of eating meat on the primary day of the week or just pick a place every day where you cook meals around beans, whole grains, and vegetables. Once you get the hang of it, try two nights every week.

Enjoy dairy products carefully. The USDA recommends limiting saturated fat to a very low 10% of your daily calories (about 200 calories for many people). It also allows you to enjoy dairy products like natural (unprocessed) cheese, Greek or plain yogurt.

For dessert, eat fresh fruit. Instead of frozen sweets, cakes, or other food, choose strawberries, fresh figs, grapes, or apples.

Use good fat. Extra-virgin vegetable oils, nuts, sunflower seeds, olives, and avocados are great sources of healthy fats for your daily diet.

What to try about mercury in fish?

Despite all the health benefits of seafood, almost all fish and shellfish have traces of pollutants, including toxic metal mercury. These guidelines can help you make the safest choice.

The concentration of mercury and other pollutants increases in larger fish, so it is best to avoid eating large fish such as sharks, swordfish, tilefish, and caveolae.

Most adults can safely eat 12 ounces (two 6-ounce servings) of other types of cooked seafood every week.

Pay attention to local seafood advice to find out if the fish you caught is safe to eat.

For pregnant, nursing mothers, and young women ages 12 and younger, choose fish and shellfish that are low in mercury, such as shrimp, salmon, canned light tuna, pollock, or catfish. Due to its high mercury content, do not eat 6 ounces (an average meal) of albacore tuna per week.

Make mealtime a social experience. The simple act of lecturing a lover or loved one on the dining table can play a big role in relieving stress and boosting mood. Eating with others can also prevent overeating; it is as healthy for your waist as it is for your attitude. Cut out the TV and computer, remove your smartphone, and hook up with someone during the meal.

Gather the family together and yet be awake with each other's daily lives. Regular family meals provide comfort to children and is an excellent thanks for keeping an eye on their eating habits as well.

Share food with others to expand your social network. If you live alone, cook a touch extra and invite a boyfriend, coworker, or neighbor to join you.

Cook with others. Invite a lover to share shopping and cooking responsibilities for Mediterranean food. Cooking with others is often thanks to deepening relationships and dividing prices, it can be cheaper for both of you.

Quick Start for Mediterranean Diet

The easiest thanks to making changes are to start with small steps. You will do this:

- Cook in vegetable oil instead of butter.
- Enjoying salads as a starter or Antrim, eating more fruits and vegetables, snacking on fruits, and incorporating veggies into other dishes.
- Choosing whole grains instead of refined bread, pasta, and rice.
- Replacement of fish at least twice per week for meat.
- Limit high-fat dairy by switching to 2% or milk skim or 1% milk

Chapter 3: Example of A Balanced Meal Plan and Useful Tips That Will Help You Every Day

This chapter includes various dietetic menus and delicious Mediterranean based dishes to prepare for breakfast, lunch and dinner

4-Week Mediterranean Diet Meal Plan

Week n.1

Breakfast (219 calories)

1 Serving Rainbow Frittata

AM Snack (62 calories)

1 Medium Orange

Lunch (374 calories)

1 Serving Salad Pisa Bread and Hummus

PM Snack (126 calories)

1 Cup Raspberries

1/4 Cup Whole Milk Greek Yogurt

Dinner (442 calories)

1 Green Bean Pilaf sat Sejong Summon Serving

Daily Total: 1,222 calories, 68 grams protein, 114 grams carbohydrates, 29 grams fiber, 58 grams fat, 1,615 mg of sodium.

Week n.2

Breakfast (287 calories)

1 Serving Raspberry

AM Snack (30 calories)

1 Plum

Lunch (337 calories)

Muesli

1 Serve Brussels Sprouts Salad with Crispy Chickpeas

PM Snack (102 calories)

2 Tbsp. Hummus

2 Medium Carrot

Dinner (479 calories)

1 Serving with Creamy Sauce

Daily Total: 1,235 calories, 45 grams of protein, 165 grams of carbohydrate, 39 grams of fiber, 48 grams of fat, 1,059 mg of sodium.

Week n.3

Breakfast (252 calories)

1 Serving of Figs and Ricotta Toast

AM Snack (61 calories),

2 Plums

Lunch (337 calories)

1 Serving Brussels Sprouts Salad with Crispy Compass

PM Snack (126 calories)

1 Cup Raspberries

1/4 Cup Whole Milk Yogurt

Dinner (429 calories)

1 Serving Tomato White Susman Cod

1 Cup Basic Quinoa

Daily Total: 1,205 calories, 59 g protein, 138 g carbohydrate, 33 g fiber, 47 g fat, 1,129 mg sodium.

Week n.4

Breakfast (291 calories)

1 Creamy Blueberry One pecan morning Jimi Service

AM Snack (62 calories)

1 Medium Orange

Lunch (337 calories)

1 Serving Brussels Sprouts Crispy Chips

Dinner (477 calories)

1 Serving Mediterranean Cycle Minister of Vince Bowl

Daily Total: 1,227 calories, 36 g protein, 159 g carbohydrate, 32 g fiber, 54 grams of fat, 1,170 mg sodium.

7-Days Mediterranean Diet Meal Plan

Day 1

Breakfast topped with Greek yoga berries and a drizzle of honey with some almond kinase

Lunch with a small breakfast small bowl of olives in a small bowl

Dinner with a hot cereal on the pigeon breast, the step zucchini, Tomatoes, and frost.

Day 2

Breakfast Kea soft boiled egg Arca with grain toast with some pistachio

Lunch roasted peppers, sun-dried tomatoes, Salsa lentils food Seth Doha capers, severity balsamic vinaigrette

Dinner eat quinoa and Saturated fried garlic

Day 3

Breakfast is whipped with ricotta walnuts and fruits topped with breakfast roasted chickpeas

Lunch whole-grain pita with double meal tabbouleh salad

Dinner Gnocchi and Roasted Chicken

Day 4

Breakfast Caprese with a few pieces of Baked Nuts Fruit

Lunch Outsized Salad with Condensed Bottle Brie

Dinner Salad Pisa Bread and Hummus

Day 5

Breakfast Cashews and Edible Fruits Beautiful

Lunch Whole Grain Rolls with Breakfast Olive Plate Flavor with Marmite, Cheese, Cucumbers, and Cherry Tomatoes some slices

Dinner cooked at the White McLeish oil and garlic, Sialkot zucchini, and sweet potato.

Day 6

Breakfast with scrambled eggs and veggies chives Lue and topped with feta bread slices of whole grain

Snack Greek yogurt

Lunch Chopped chicken, feta, and topped with veggies.

Snack Hummus with Cakes

Dinner Grilled Seafood, Roasted Fennel and Broccoli, Arugula Salad, and Quinoa.

Day 7

Breakfast Veggie Frittata

Snack Some Berries

Lunch a Plate of Salmon, Capers, Lemon, Whole Grain Crackers, and Raw Vegetable

Snack Avocado with lemon and salt. Cucumber

Dinner red sauce and mussels with pasta.

Chapter 4: Mediterranean Diet Breakfast Recipes

Mediterranean Breakfast Board

Ingredients

- 1 Falafel Recipe
- 1 Classic Hummus Recipe (or Roasted Garlic Hummus, Roasted Red Chili)

- Hummus Baba Ghanoush Recipe
- Feta Cheese or 1 Labneh Recipe
- 1 tabbouleh Recipe
- 1 to 2 Tomatoes, sliced
- 1 English cucumber, sliced
- 7 to 6 radishes, half-sliced
- Mixed olives (I like a mixture of green olives and kalamata olives
- Spiced artichokes or mushrooms
- Early Harvest EVOO and Zaatar Dip
- Garnish taka pita roti, chopped
- Grapes (palette cleanser)

Instructions

- Harmonize Falafel with this recipe. You must start at least the night before soaking the chickpeas. See the notes below for further work. (You can also buy in an area of Middle Eastern store.) Make
- Hamas with Falafels recipe and Baba Ganesh is in line with this recipe. You will prepare them both the night before and store them inside the fridge. If you want, try turning roasted garlic hummus or roasted red chili hummus into different things. (If you don't have time, use quality store-bought hummus.)

- Prepare sliced feta cheese, or premature labneh to suit this recipe.
- Make a table with this recipe. Often made a few days in advance and refrigerated in tight-lid glass containers.
- To assemble a Mediterranean breakfast board, place hummus, baba Ganesh, olive oil, zaatar, tabbouleh in the bowl. To create the focus, place the most important bowl in the middle of an excluded wooden board or platter. Arrange the remaining bowls on individual parts of the board to create movement or shape. Use the gap between the bowls to add the remaining ingredients such as falafel, chopped vegetables, and beaten bread. Add garnish with grapes and fresh herbs if you wish.

Note:

Pro Tip: If you propose to make the most of it from scratch, start a few nights before. The most effort will be made to organize falafel (unless you are buying a falafel prepared from a Middle Eastern store.) But you can easily make falafel patties and freeze them in advance if you want, so fry or bake. Before assembling them (from Frozen), the breakfast board. See the full Falafel tutorial and recipe notes here.

Pro tip: Hummus, Baba Ganesh, and Taboola can also be prepared an evening or two in advance. Store within the fridge in a tight-lid glass container.

Pro tip: Visit the deli section (many also have olive bars) of your local grocery store to look for mixed olives and pickled items. You will use marinated artichokes, mushrooms, roasted red pepper, etc.

Pro tip: If you want to feature an excluded egg dish next to the current board to finish your brunch party, consider Sukuk, spinach frittata, or this Mediterranean egg casserole.

Recommended for this recipe: Early Harvest Extra virgin vegetable oil (from organically grown and processed Cornice olives) and all-natural guitars for dipping.

Egg Baked

Ingredients

4 servings

- 2 tablespoons vegetable oil
- 8 medium tomatoes
- 8 large eggs

- ¼ cup milk
- ¼ cup grated Parmesan cheese
- Salt and freshly ground black pepper
- 4 tablespoons fresh chopped herbs (parsley, thyme, rosemary Roof a mixture

Instructions

1. Preheat oven to 375 ° F. Lubricates an outdoor, oven-safe pan with vegetable oil.
2. Employing a small Perry, rounding the tomato stems and taking them away. Use a spoon to flush out all the insides of the tomato. (Reserve the Ingrid's and use them to make spaghetti sauce or salsa.)
3. Arrange the tomato shells neatly inside the prepared skillet. Break an egg into each tomato. Top each egg with 1 tablespoon milk and 1 teaspoon Parmesan. Season each egg with salt and pepper.
4. Bake until tomatoes are soft, egg white sets in, and so yolks are still a touch for 15 to 17 minutes. Let cool for 5 minutes then garnish with fresh herbs. Serve immediately.

Quinoa Breakfast Chili

Ingredients

- 4 chopped coarsely chopped bacon, chopped
- 1 small sweet potato, chopped
- 1/2 purple onion, chopped
- 1/2 red pepper, sliced
- 1/2 sweet pepper,

- 1 cup chopped mushrooms, Chopped
- 2 garlic cloves, minced meat.
- 1/2 cup uncooked quinoa, rinsed
- 1 cup low-sodium vegetable or chicken broth or water
- 4 eggs, to taste your essential
- Way salt and pepper

Instructions

- Heat an outsized pan over medium heat and add bacon. Cook until the fat is rendered, and the bacon is crispy, then remove the bacon with a slotted spoon and place it on a towel to empty. Reduce heat to medium and add sweet potato, onion, chili, mushrooms, and garlic to the sweet potato to coat. Cover and cook for 5-6 minutes, stirring once or twice until soft.
- Add the uncooked quinoa to the vegetables and shake for 1-2 minutes so that it becomes lightly toasted. Add available or water and bring the mixture to a boil. Reduce to a boil immediately, cover, and cook for 15-ish minutes until the quinoa is cooked through. While the quinoa is cooking, prepare the eggs at will. Once cooked, taste and season to your liking. Serve quinoa in the bowl with eggs and cooked bacon.

Savory Steel Cut Oatmeal

- **Ingredients**
- 3 cups of water
- 1 cup neutral-flavored milk is preferred or another cup of water
- 1 tbsp unsalted butter or vegetable

- 1 cup steel-cut oats (certified Select gluten) -If Oates necessary)
- More teaspoon to taste salt freshly ground black Marc Bhanu, flavor
- Mix-ins Charlene cheese or nutritional yeast, extra Vans End Oil drizzle or butter, Subedar vegetables or herbs, bunches of dried tomatoes, red peppers in the sun and/or ground spices
- Topping ideas: the chopped nuts or seeds, and / Kutak fried / Scrambled eggs and/or freshly prepared fresh greens.

Instructions

- In a large saucepan combines water and milk. Bring the mixture to a boil over medium heat. Meanwhile, melt the butter or heat the vegetable oil during a 12-inch skillet during medium heat. Once the butter ceases or the oil starts to flicker, add the oats and cook, shaking occasionally, golden and fragrant, about 2 minutes. This toasting step greatly enhances the taste of oats.
- Stir the oats in the water/milk mixture. Reduce the heat to medium-low and simmer gently for about 20 to 25 minutes, until the mixture becomes very thick.
- Stir within the salt. Still, boil the mixture, shake occasionally, and reduce the heat required to stop the scorching on the rock

bottom until most of the liquid is absorbed about 10 minutes. (If you have doubled the recipe, your oatmeal may require 5 minutes of extra time to cook here.) When this is done, the oatmeal is going to be very creamy.

- Remove from heat and let the oatmeal rest for five minutes before serving so that it thickens and reduces the temperature of the palate—season to taste with extra salt (I added another taste spoon), pepper, and optional spices. Stir in any mix-ins you want now.
- Add oatmeal to the oatmeal bowl and any toppings you want. Allow cooling completely before covering any excess oatmeal and cooling.

Hummus and Vegetables Breakfast Bowl

Ingredients

Breakfast Ingredients Bowls:

- 1 tbsp avocado oil or vegetable oil
- 1 lb. asparagus, dog bite-size pieces (trimmed with ends and discarded)

- 3 cups chopped cabbage leaves
- 1 batch yellow little dressing
- 3 cups chopped (uncooked) Brussels sprouts[2]
- 1 hum cup cooked Quinoa Avocado
- ½ cup hummus
- 1 peel of, peel a thin-thin-thin
- 4 eggs, cooked you (I soft-boiled mine) however
- Guarantee Niche will: The sunflower seeds (or chopped almonds), are crushed sesame seeds.
- Black Pepper

Dressing Ingredients:
- 2 tablespoons avocado oil or vegetable oil
- 2 tablespoons freshly squeezed juice
- 2 tablespoons Dijon mustard
- 1 clove, minced
- Salt and fresh firecrackers Chili

Instructions:

- Oil warm medium to large over a large High heat during sauté pan. Add asparagus and sauté for 4-5 minutes, occasionally stirring, until tender. Remove from heat and set side to side.
- Meanwhile, during a large bowl, combine the banana and lemon dressing. Then using your fingers, massage the dressing into the bud for 2-3 minutes or until the leaves turn

black and soft. Add Brussels sprouts, quinoa, and cooked asparagus, and toss until combined.

- To assemble the bowl, smear a spoon of hummus over the side of each bowl. Then place the kale salad evenly in the middle of four bowls, topped with avocado, egg, and your required garnish. Serve immediately.
- To make Lemon Vinaigrette: Mix all ingredients together during a small bowl until combined.

Banana Mocha Overnight Oats

Ingredients

- 1 banana
- 3/4 cup almond milk or another non-dairy milk of choice
- 1/2 cup strong coffee cold drink well

- Served 2 pitted dates. If your blender is not very strong, you can hear it in Soak water for one hour, then drain before mixing
- 2 tablespoons chocolate
- Pinch sea salt
- 1 cup oatmeal
- 1 1/2 teaspoon chia seeds to serve fresh fruit

Instructions

- Together banana, almond milk, Mix coffee, dates, chocolate, and sea salt until smooth during a blender. Keep oats and chia seeds in an airtight container.
- Pour the liquid mixture over the oats and chia seeds, then stir everything to blend well. Cover overnight and refrigerate.
- In the morning, shake your oats again and sprinkle a little bit of extra non-dairy milk as necessary. Top with fresh fruit and luxuriate.

Avocado with Ketogenic Baked Eggs and Muddles

Ingredients

2 serving

- 3 Zucchini to garnish spiralized in noodles, garnishing
- 2 tablespoons of vegetable oil 2
- kosher salt and freshly ground pepper
- 4 large eggs
- Red-pepper flakes,
- Fresh Basil. Half and finely chopped

Instructions

1. Preheat oven to 350 ° F. Lightly grease the baking sheet with nonstick spray.

2. During a large bowl, combine zucchini noodles and vegetable oil. Season with salt and pepper. Divide the 4 into even parts, transfer to a baking sheet and shape each into a nest.

3. Gently break an egg in the middle of each nest. Bake for 9 to 11 minutes until eggs are set. Season with salt and pepper; garnish with red chili flakes and basil. Serve with avocado slices.

Breakfast Jar

Ingredients

- 1 yellow bell pepper
- 1 red bell pepper
- 1/2 cup hummus
- 1/2 cup guacamole
- 1/2 cup grape tomato

- Fist snipe crisps
- 1/2 cup strawberries
- 1/2 cup plain Greek yogurt 1/2
- 1 cup Granola
- 1/4 cup blueberries
- 1/2 cup spread
- 2 celery stalks
- 1/2 cup pretzel
- Pins mason jar with lids

Instructions

- Prepare the first jar of bell pepper and hummus. Slice peppers into 1/4-inch strips. Use a spoon to layer in hummus, then top with slices of bell pepper. Seal it and store it in the fridge.
- Prepare a jar of guacamole and turtle bean crisps. Layer in Guacamole first, add in tomatoes for the center layer, then top with Harvest Snaps Turtle Bean Han borough Crisps. Seal it and store it in the fridge. (You want to eat this snack within 24 hours, so not getting crispy.)
- Prepare the perfect jar. Sliced Strawberries. Layer in yogurt, granola, strawberries, and blueberries. Seal it and store it in the fridge.
- Prepare spread and celery jar. Cut celery stalks into 3-inch slices. The crust extends to the bottom of the rock, add to the crudités, and top with pretzels. Seal it and store it in the fridge.

- You want to eat this snack within 24-48 hours, so pretzels are not disgusting.
- Grab your snacks as necessary, whether you are on the way or need a bite to eat a day. Enjoy it!

Chapter 5: Mediterranean Diet Lunch Recipes

Mediterranean Chicken Tacos

Ingredients

- 8 soft taco shells
- 2-3 chicken breasts to be melted and bite-size pieces

- 1/2 cup grape tomatoes chopped
- 1/4 cup purple onion sliced
- 2/3 cup feta cheese
- 1 cup hummus store or seeds of this recipe minus the mole

Tzatziki Sauce:

- 6 cloves of garlic
- 1/2 cup cucumber
- Juice 1/2 Nimbus
- 2 tablespoons fresh dill
- 2 mint leaves
- 1/2 cup plain Greek yogurt
- Salt and black Microwave

Instructions

- 1-2 tablespoons of oil Heat an outsized pan with Bake, the chicken in skillet.
- When the chicken is cooking, make the tzatziki sauce and hence the humus. For Tzatziki Sauce: Combine garlic, cucumber, lemon, dill, and mint during a blender and pulse for 5–10 seconds. Pour into a bowl and stir in the curd by hand until everything is combined; put aside.
- While the chicken is cooking, cut the tomatoes and onions.
- Once the chicken is done, pour it into a bowl of tzatziki sauce and shake until the chicken is well coated.

- Heat the taco shells during a pan until hot, then fill them with hummus, chicken, and vegetables.
- Enjoy it!

Mediterranean Quinoa Bowls with Roasted Red Poivrade

Ingredients

- 1 16 oz jar Roasted Red Peppers, drained (or fry your own red peppers and win a medal game!)
- 1 clove garlic
- 1/2 teaspoon salt (more to taste)
- 1 lemon juice!
- ½ Vanaspati oil
- 1/2 cup almonds for

- Mediterranean bowls (build your own bowls to support what you like)
- Cooked quinoa
- Spinach, cabbage, yucca kalamata
- Feta cheese
- Olives
- Pepperoncini
- Thinly sliced onions violet
- Hummus
- Fresh basil or parsley
- Olive oil, juice, salt, pepper

Instructions

- Pour all ingredients to the sauce while mostly smooth until a kitchen appliance or blender. Looks should be thick and textured.
- Cook the quinoa according to the package directions (I always do mine during the rice cooker while I buy everything prepared). When the quinoa is complete, make yourself a Mediterranean quinoa bowl!
- Store leftovers in separate containers and assemble each bowl before serving, especially greens, and so sauces, as they will all soften when stored with the opposite ingredients.

Greek Lemon Soup

Ingredients

- 2 tablespoons vegetable oil, divided into
- 1-pound boneless, skinless chicken thighs, 1-inch bran
- kosher salt and freshly ground black pepper
- 4 cloves garlic, minced garlic,
- 3 carrots, peeled and
- 2 stalks Warm celery. Cut

- 1/2 teaspoon thyme
- 8 cups chicken broth
- 2 bay leaves
- 2 (15.5 oz) cans cannellini beans, rinsed and dried
- 4 cups baby spinach
- 2 tablespoons for fresh flavoring, squeezed more juice, or 2 tablespoons chopped crown Parsley leaves
- 2 tbsp chopped fresh dill

Instructions

- Heat 1 tbsp of vegetable oil on medium heat during a large stockpot or Dutch oven. Season chicken thighs to taste with salt and pepper. Add chicken to the stockpot and cook until golden, about 2-3 minutes; put aside.
- Add the remaining 1 tbsp oil to the stockpot. Add garlic, onions, carrots, and celery. Cook, occasionally stirring, until tender, about 3-4 minutes. Stir in the thyme for about 1 minute.
- Whisk in chicken broth and bay leaves. Bring back a boil; Reduce heat in the cannellini beans and chicken and occasionally shake, until slightly thickened, about 10–15 minutes.
- Stir in spinach, about 2 minutes. Stir in the juice, parsley, and dill, season with salt and pepper to taste.
- Serve immediately

Greek Fetus Salad

Ingredients

Salad:

- 2 whole wheat ground or flatbread rounds (white also works fine)
- 2 tablespoons vegetable oil
- 1/4 teaspoon coarse salt
- 4 cups chopped romaine lettuce This
- medium cucumber, peeled, quarter, and Chopped
- 1 yellow bell pepper., Digging 3/4-inch chicks
- 1/2-pint (1 cup) cherry tomatoes, half
- 1/2 small purple onions, finely chopped

- 1/2 cup flat Italian parsley leaves
- 1/2 cup kalamata olives,
- 3/4 cups for the laminated feta cheese

Dressing:
- 1/3 cup vegetable oil
- 2 tablespoons wine vinegar
- 1 small clove garlic, minced
- 1/2 teaspoon oregano
- 1/4 teaspoon coarse salt
- 1/8 teaspoon fresh pepper

Instructions

- Oven Preheat to 350 ° F.
- Cut the slices in half and place them on a baking sheet. Bake once, until golden brown and toasted, for 10–15 minutes. Let cool. Cut the cut gall bladder into pieces (1-inch). Add them to a medium bowl and drizzle over the bread with 2 tablespoons of vegetable oil. Toss to coat. Sprinkle with kosher salt and toss again to distribute.
- In an outside bowl, add lettuce, cucumber, bell peppers, tomatoes, onions, parsley, and olives. Toss.
- Create a vignette. In a small bowl, add 1/3 cup vegetable oil, vinegar, garlic, parsley, salt, and pepper. Unless mixed.

- Add pieces of ground bread and so beat the salad. Drizzle vinaigrette at most. Toss gently to mix. Serve immediately.

Harissa Salad

Ingredients

- 1 1/2 lbs. baby potato (leave the skins)
- 2 tbsp harissa paste
- 6 ounces low-fat or nonfat Greek yogurt
- 1/4 tsp. Salt

- 1/4 teaspoon. Black pepper
- Juice 1 lemon
- 1/4 cup finely cooked onions
- 1/4 cup fresh cilantro or parsley, roughly chopped

Instructions

- Place the potatoes in a large pot and put them in 1-1 to 2 inches of cold, salted water. Mix. Bring water to a boil over medium-high heat. The potatoes are then cooked, uncovered until they are fork for about 9–11 minutes. Dry the potatoes and set them aside to cool slightly.
- Meanwhile, a small bowl of whiskey with harissa, Greek yogurt, salt, pepper, and juice.
- Transfer the still-hot potatoes to an outside bowl. Add the dressing and bend it gently until the potato is well coated. Then carefully fold in the dried purple onions and herbs.
- Serve immediately when heated to temperature or even after cooling.
- The leftovers are often stored in an airtight container in your refrigerator for 2-3 days.

Greek Quinoa Bowls

Ingredients

- 1 cup quinoa
- 1.5 cups water
- 1 cup chopped green bell pepper
- 1 cup chopped red bell chopped

- 1/3 cup feta cheese
- 1/4 cup extra virgin vegetable oil
- 2-3 TBSP apple vinegar
- Salt and Swarna pepper to
- 12 tbsp fresh parsley

Instructions

- Rinse first and a mesh strainer to your quinoa Education facilities in the working sieve.
- Bring a medium saucepan to medium heat and lightly toast the quinoa to get rid of any excess water. Stir as it just bangs for a minute or two. This step is optional but adds the nutritional and full factor of quinoa!
- Next, add your water, set the burner to high, and bring to a boil.
- Once boiling, reduce the heat to low and simmer, cover with a lid, a little azure, for 12–13 minutes or until the quinoa is fluffy, and therefore the liquid has been absorbed.
- While the quinoa cooks, chop and prepare the remaining ingredients and mix their dressing ingredients together.
- Smell your now-fluffing quinoa from the pot and provide a touch of fluff with a fork.
- For a comfort salad, you'll pop the quinoa within the fridge for a few minutes before adding your vegetables or simply let it

cool on the countertop for an area temperature quinoa bowl. Totally up to you!
- For a super simple vinaigrette, mix vegetable oil, apple vinegar, salt, and pepper together. How easy it was!? Pour over your quinoa bowl and toss with a pair of forks or salad servers and dig in.

Faroe Second with Ronnie Grease Chicken and Oven Fries

Ingredients

- 1-pound boneless chicken breast
- 2 tbsp extra virgin vegetable oil
- 2 vinegar vinegar
- 1 tbsp fresh dill
- 1 tbsp chopped fresh parsley
- 1 tbsp paprika
- 2 cloves garlic, minced or grated
- Kosher salt and pepper
- 1-pound Russet Potatoes, Digi dies.

- 1–2 red bell peppers, chopped
- 2 cups cooked faro, or other ancient grains of
- 1 head butter lettuce, roughly torn
- 8 ounces of feta, cubed
- Tzatziki (or yogurt), olives, cucumbers, red onions, for serving.
- Red wine
- 1/4cup extra Virgin NSPA oil
- 3 tablespoons wine vinegar
- 1 tablespoon honey
- 1 Nausea juice
- 1 tablespoon chopped fresh oregano
- 1-2 cloves garlic, minced Yams
- 1 cluster pinch crushed red pepper
- Kosher salt and pepper

Instructions

- Preheat 425 F Karen oven sheet, degrees2 Hua. Ak ripe baking chicken, 1 tablespoon vegetable oil, Balsamic vinegar, dill, oregano, blood In, and add an external pinch of both salt and pepper. Toss well to coat the chicken evenly. Add potatoes, and bell peppers, and toss with the remaining 1 tbsp of vegetable oil and a pinch of both salt and pepper. Arrange everything in a nice layer. Fry for 40-45 minutes, cook till half cooked until the chicken is cooked, and hence the potatoes turn golden. Allow the chicken to cool slightly and then add to the chunks.

- To assemble: smear the bottom of a salad tzatziki 4 rock salad bowl. Add Ferro, lettuce, bell paper, potato, and chicken. Sprinkle fatter and top as desired with olives, cucumber, and purple onions. Drizzle with wine vinaigrette (recipe is as follows).
- Red Wine Vinaigrette, combine all ingredients during a bowl or glass jar. Mix well. Taste and adjust seasonings as needed.

Wild Alaskan Salmon and Smoked Cucumber Cereal Bowls

Ingredients

4 servings

- 2 cups Faro
- 2 Lemon Juice
- 2 tablespoons Dijon Mustard
- 1 Clove, Minced
- Ms. Cup Plus 2 Tbsp Extra-Virgin Vegetable Oil
- Kosher Salt and Freshly Ground Pepper
- 1 European cucumber, dig - 1-inch chunks
- Chuck seasoned rice vinegar

- Chopped cup chopped fresh parsley
- ¼ cup chopped fresh mint
- 1 cup chopped fresh dill
- Four 6-ounce wild Alaskan Saw Mr. Salmon filings

Instructions

1. Bring an outer pot of salted water to a boil. Add wire to boiling water and cook until tender, 25 to half an hour. Drain.

2. Transfer the furrows to a medium bowl. Mix juice, mustard, garlic, and I've cup in olive oil, Season with salt and pepper.

3. While in a separate medium bowl, smash the cucumber pieces with a fork. Add rice vinegar and toss to mix. Season with salt and pepper, and add parsley, mint, and dill.

4. During a large pan, heat the remaining 2 tablespoons of vegetable oil over medium heat. Season the salmon with salt and pepper. Add fillets to recent oil and cook for desired doneness, 8 to 10 minutes.

5. To serve, divide the furrows among four bowls. Coarsely hack a salmon fillet and top each bowl with cucumbers and herbs.

Stuffed Brinjal

Ingredients

4 servings

- 2 medium brinjals, half a
- teaspoon vegetable oil,
- 1 onion,
- 2 garlic cloves, Hua

- 1-pint Ceremony Mushroom, quarter quinoa
- 2 cups torn
- 2 cups cooked
- 1 tablespoon chopped fresh thyme
- Zest and juice. Lemon (plus extra lemon wedge to serve)
- Salt and recently ground black pepper
- ½ cup plain Greek yogurt
- Garnished for 3 tablespoons fresh parsley chopped

Insrtructions

1. Preheat oven to 400 ° F. Line a baking sheet with parchment paper.

2. Using a spoon, scoop a 3 of the meat inside the eggplant (you can set it aside for other uses or discard). Rub half of each eggplant with 1 teaspoon vegetable oil and transfer to the prepared baking sheet.

3. Add a leftover pan over medium heat and the remaining 1 tbsp of vegetable oil to heat. Add onion and tender for 3 to 4 minutes. Add garlic and cook until fragrant, 1 minute more.

4. Add mushrooms and cook until they are just tender 4 to five minutes. Stir within the bananas and quinoa and cook until the fort is slightly subdued for 2 to three minutes. Season the mixture with thyme, lemon peel, and juice, salt, and pepper.

5. Spoon the filling into the prepared brinjals and fry the brinjals until tender, but do not fall for 17 to twenty minutes. Let cool for five minutes.

6. Serve eggplants immediately, garnish with parsley and pour between yogurt and an extra lemon wedge.

Greek Turkey Burger with Tzatziki Sauce

Ingredients

4 servings

- 1 tbsp extra virgin vegetable oil
- 1 sweet onion, minced
- 2 garlic cloves, minced

- 1 egg
- ½ cup chopped fresh parsley
- ½ teaspoon dried oregano
- ¼ teaspoon of red pepper flakes
- 1-pound ground turkey
- ¾ cup bread
- Salt and freshly ground pepper
- Crumbs Tzatziki Sauce
- 1 cup Greek
- Yogurt, European cucumber,
- 2 tablespoons juice
- 1 pinch of garlic powder,
- Salt and freshly ground black pepper
- ¼ cup chopped fresh parsley
- 4 Wheat Hamburger Buns
- Purple Onion, Sliced
- 8 Boston Salad Leaves
- 2 Tomatoes, Sliced

Instructions

1. Make a Turkey Burger: During a small bowl, heat vegetable oil over medium heat. Add onions and cook for 3 to 4 minutes, tender. Add garlic and sauté until fragrant, 1 minute more. Set aside to cool.

2. During a medium bowl, combine the cooled onion mixture with eggs, parsley, parsley, red pepper flakes, and ground turkey. Add seasonings with breadcrumbs, salt, and pepper, and mix until combined.

3. Preheat the oven to 375 ° F. Form the meat mixture into four equal-sized patties. Heat an outdoor oven-safe pan over medium-high heat and spray it liberally with non-cooking spray.

4. Place the burger within the skeleton and bake for 4 to five minutes on each side, until well browned. Transfer the skillet to the oven and cook until the burger is fully cooked 15 to 17 minutes.

5. Use Tzatziki: During a medium bowl, mix the yogurt with cucumber, olive oil, juice, and garlic powder. Season with salt and pepper, then stir within the parsley.

6. Make the toppings: Place each burger on a rock bottom half bun, then each with a cup of tea tiki, two lettuce leaves, two tomato slices, and so the top half-bun. Serve immediately.

Eggplant Pizza

Ingredients

6 servings

- 1 large (or 2 medium) eggplant
- 1 cups vegetable oil
- Salt and freshly ground black pepper ground
- 1 cup marinara sauce (store-bought or homemade)
- 2 cups chopped mozzarella cheese
- 2 cups cherry tomatoes, half a

- 1 cup of torn Basil leaves

Instructions

1. Preheat oven to 400 ° F. Line a baking sheet with parchment paper.

2. Cut the loops with the brinjal (s), then dig into inch thick slices. Arrange the slices on the prepared baking sheet and brush each side of each slice with vegetable oil—season with salt and pepper.

3. Fry the eggplant slices for about 10 to 12 minutes.

4. Remove the tray from the oven and spread 2 tablespoons of marinara sauce on top of each slice. Top generously with mozzarella and arrange 3 to five cherry tomato pieces on each top.

5. Return the pizza to the oven and fry until the cheese melts, and so the tomatoes are blistered for 5 to 7 minutes.

6. Heat the pizza, garnish with basil.

Greek Lemon Chicken with Tzatziki Soak

Ingredients

- Tzatziki sauce
- 1 cup Greek yogurt
- Half European Mkhitar, chopped

- 1 tablespoon extra-virgin vegetable oil
- 2 tablespoons juice,
- Garlic powder Keeping
- Salt and fresh ground black pepper
- ¼ cup fresh chopped dill

- ¼ cup Greek yogurt
- Zest and juice of 1 lemon
- 1 teaspoon dried oregano
- 1 teaspoon garlic powder
- pinch salt
- 1 Skin pounds boneless skinless pigeon breast, digging ½-inch Turpitude
- Castro-virgin vegetable oil,
- salt and freshly ground black pepper
- ¼ cup chopped fresh parsley.

Instructions

1. Make Tzatziki: During a medium bowl, mix the yogurt with cucumber, olive oil, juice, and garlic powder. Season with salt and pepper to taste, then stir within the dill.

2. Make Skewers: In a small bowl, mix the curd with lemon peel, juice, parsley, garlic powder, and cayenne.

3. During a separate bowl, rub the chicken with the yogurt-lemon mixture to coat it well.

4. Place a piece of chicken on each skewer, weaving the bandage back and forth as you thread it over the skewer to secure it.

5. Brush the skewer on each side with vegetable oil, then season with salt and pepper, working in batches, cook on a preheated grill or grill pan until well blended on each side, 4 to five minutes per side

6. Serve immediately, garnish with parsley and tzatziki sauce on the side.

Salmon Bowl Faro, Black Beans and Tahini Dressing

Ingredients

1 serving

- 2 tablespoons tahini
- Jest and 1 lemon juice
- East spoon turmeric, split
- Powder spoon garlic powder
- Tablespoon extra-virgin vegetable oil
- Kosher salt and freshly ground black pepper

- ¼ cup Farrow
- ½ cup black beans cooked
- ½ teaspoon cumin
- 6 ounces salmon
- 1½ teaspoons smoked paprika
- ½ teaspoon coriander
- 4 Boston salad leaves
- ½ avocado, chopped thinly
- 2 scallions thinly sliced
- ¼ Fresno Chili, thinly sliced

Instructions

1. During a small bowl, gently tahini, lemon peel, juice, turmeric, spoon, and so garlic powder together. Gradually add 3 tablespoons of vegetable oil and whisk until the dressing becomes thick and well emulsified—season with salt and pepper.

2. Bring the thyme and 1 cup of water in a small pot during medium heat. Reduce the heat to low and simmer for 20 to 25 minutes until the tender is extremely low.

3. Mix beans, 1 tablespoon of vegetable oil, and so cumin during a small bowl.

4. Season the salmon with smoked paprika, coriander, remaining with spoon turmeric, salt, and pepper—heat 2 tbsp of vegetable oil in a medium-sized nonstick pan on medium heat. Add salmon

and cook, undisturbed, until one side is browned and just opaque within the center, about 5 minutes.

5. Place the lettuce leaves within the base of your serving bowl. Top with Faro, black beans, and salmon. Garnish with avocado, scallions, and chopped chile, Drizzle with dressing.

Toasted Zaatar Pita Bread with Mezze Plater

Ingredients

4 servings

- 4 wheat pita rounds
- 4 tablespoons extra virgin vegetable oil
- 4 tablespoons zaatar
- 1 cup yogurt Greek
- Kosher salt and freshly ground black pepper
- 1 cup hummus

- 1 cup spicy artichoke hearts
- 1 cup chopped Roasted Red Peppers
- 2 Cups Mixed Olives

- 2 Cups Cherry Tomatoes
- 4 Ounce Salami

Instructions

1. Heat an outdoor pan over medium-high heat. Brush each side of each pyre with vegetable oil and season with cumin.

2. Working in batches, add pistachios to the pan and toast until golden brown, about 2 minutes per side. Slice each beaten into quarters.

3. Season Greek yogurt with salt and pepper.

4. To divide Pisa, Greek Yogurt, Hummus, Artichoke Hearts, Roasted Red Peppers, Olives, Tomatoes, and Salami among four plates.

Pesto Quinoa Bowls with Roasted Vegetables and Labneh

Ingredients

4 servings

- 1 large Japanese eggplant, cubed,
- 1 medium zucchini cubed
- 1-pint cherry tomatoes, sliced

- Romano (or green) beans in half
- extra virgin vegetable oil
- Kosher salt and fresh ground black pepper
- 1 cup quinoa, rinsed
- Half bought your favorite pesto cup (either homemade or store)
- Labneh 1 cup of Greek yogurt
- 1 minced clove
- Half N Busters
- Coriander or parsley Kempt Over (or both!) Roughly chopped

Instructions

1. Before baking with oven parchment paper hot 400 degrees baking sheet and eggplant, zucchini, cherry tomatoes and Arrange the beans. Apply vegetable oil with salt and pepper to the vegetable oil. Fry until all the vegetables are tender and caramelized, for 30 to 40 minutes.

2. Meanwhile, add quinoa to a medium saucepan with 2 cups of water and a pinch of salt. Bring back to a boil, cover, reduce to a boil, and cook for a quarter-hour. After the quinoa cooking is complete, remove the lid, fluff it with a fork, and allow it to chill. Once the quinoa has cooled slightly, toss it with the pesto.

3. Whisk the labneh, garlic, juice, and herbs together during a small bowl.

4. Gather each bowl by adding quinoa and arrange the vegetables in rows to look like a rainbow. Then add a dollop of Labneh on the arm.

Mediterranean Couscous with Tuna and Pepperoncini

Ingredients

4 servings

- 1 cup chicken stock or water
- 1 ¼ cup couscous
- ¾ teaspoon kosher salt

- two 5-ounce cans oil pack tuna
- 1-pint cherry tomatoes,
- ½ cup chopped pepperoncini
- ⅓ cup chopped fresh parsley
- ¼ cup capers
- Extra virgin vegetable oil serves 1.
- Kosher salt and freshly ground black pepper
- 1 lemon, quartered

Instructions

1. Make Kukus: a little break over the pot Medium heat for broth or watering. Remove the pot from the heat, stir inside and canopy the pot. Let sit for 10 minutes.

2. Make accompaniments: Meanwhile, in a medium bowl, toss together the tuna, tomato, pepperoni, parsley, and capers.

3. Fluff the cuffs with a fork, season with salt and pepper, and drizzle with vegetable oil. Top with couscous with tuna mixture and serve with lemon wedges.

Herbs Flatbread

Ingredients

- Eggplant Lebanon dip tahini
- 2 lbs. eggplant
- 6 cloves garlic,
- East teaspoon ground cumin
- p spoon Paprika
- 2 tablespoons vegetable oil

- 1 tablespoon juice
- ¼ cup tahini
- Kosher salt taste
- 1/2-pound pizza dough
- 1 bunch Scalloped sliced slices. At a hard angle
- 1 big some peppermint parsley and basil leaves
- 1 tbsp juice
- Kosher salt and freshly cracked black pepper to taste
- Olive
- 1 cup feta crumbled

Instructions

- Brush the eggplant everywhere with a fork. Boil them until all the sides of the skin turn black and soften them. Place eggplant in a bowl and canopy with wrap. Set aside to cool for 45 minutes.
- Peel the eggplants and cut the skins, discard the skin, and grow in a large clean bowl.
- Finely chop garlic, add a pinch of salt. Increase the eggplant. Add cumin, paprika, vegetable oil, and juice to the eggplants and stir to mix. Add tahini, stir to mix. Taste and adjust salt and juice as needed.
- Preheat oven to 450 ° F on a lightly floured the surface to roll a thin layer of dough about the dimensions of a sheet pan. Transfer to an oiled baking sheet, drizzle with vegetable oil.

8–12 min until golden. Remove from the oven and slow down with eggplant mixture.

- In a small bowl, combine mint, parsley, and basil and toss with the juice, salt, and pepper. Drizzle with vegetable oil and toss. Add the herb mixture over the eggplant layer and finish with feta. Serve immediately.

Mini Chicken Shawarma

Ingredients

8 servings

Chicken:

- 1-pound chicken tenders
- ¼ cup extra virgin vegetable oil
- Jest and 1 lemon juice
- 2 teaspoons garlic powder
- 1 teaspoon ground cumin
- ¾ teaspoon ground coriander

- ½ teaspoon smoked paprika
- 1 teaspoon fresh ground black pepper

Sauce:
- 1 ¼ cup Greek yogurt
- 1 tablespoon juice
- 1 clove, grated
- Popped cup chopped fresh parsley
- 2 tablespoons chopped fresh dill
- Kosher had salt and fresh ground pepper
- On banks, Ni finely chopped
- 4 leaves the Rom Chida, chopped
- ½ English cucumber, finely thin
- 1 onion
- 2 tomatoes, chopped
- 16 Mini beats. Bread

Instructions

1. 1. Make Chicken: Place chicken in a large resealable bag. During a small bowl, mix vegetable oil, lemon peel, juice, garlic powder, cumin, coriander, paprika, and black pepper together. Pour marinade in the bag, seal, and toss the chicken to coat well. Marinate the chicken for half an hour to 1 hour.

2. Make sauce: Chicken marinades, shake Greek yogurt, juice, and garlic together during a medium bowl. Stir within parsley and dill, season with salt and pepper, cover and chill.

3. Heat an outdoor pan over medium heat. Remove the chicken from the surplus, allow the surplus to drip, and cook until it browns well on each side and is fully cooked, about 4 minutes per side. Cut it into bite-size strips.

4. To assemble, divide chicken, onion, lettuce, cucumber, and tomato equally into fathers.

Greek Chicken and Rice Skillet

Ingredients

4/6 servings

- 6 chicken thighs
- Kosher salt and freshly ground black pepper
- 1 teaspoon dried parsley

- 1 teaspoon garlic powder
- 3 lemons
- 2 tablespoons extra-virgin vegetable oil
- ½ purple onion, minced
- 2 garlic cloves, Minced
- 1 cup long. -Grain rice
- 2½ cups chicken stock
- chopped 1 tbsp fresh oregano, plus
- 1 cup of green olives and
- 1/2 cup of broken feta cheese
- ½ cup fresh chopped fresh parsley

Instructions

1. Preheat oven to 375 ° F more. Season the chicken thighs with salt and pepper. During a small bowl, stir together with a mixture of dried oregano, garlic powder, and 1 lemon. Rub the mixture evenly over the chicken.

2. Heat vegetable oil during a large oven-safe pan over medium heat. Add the chicken, down the skin side, and until the chicken is well browned, 7 to 9 minutes. Remove and reserve on a plate.

3. Add onion and garlic to the pan and cook until translucent, about 5 minutes. Stir inside the rice and sauce for 1 minute, Season with salt.

4. Add chicken stock and bring the mixture to a boil. Stir within the fresh oregano and hence the juicy lemon juice. Slice the remaining 2 lemons and keep aside.

5. Nestle the chicken, skin side in the rice mixture. Transfer the skillet to the oven and cook until the rice absorbs all the liquid and so the chicken is fully cooked 20 to 25 minutes.

6. Activate the broiler and arrange the lemon slices on top of the chicken. Boil the skillet until the lemon turns a light color, and so the chicken skin is very crisp about 3 minutes.

7. Add olives and feta to the bowl, garnish with fresh parsley and serve immediately.

Grilled Lemon-Herb Chicken and Avocado Salad

Ingredients

4 servings

Lemon-Herb Chicken:

- 1 CH pounds Boneless, Skinless Chicken Breasts
- 3 Tbsp Extra-Virgin Vegetable Oil
- Zest and Juice Two Lemon Juice
- 1 Tbsp Chopped Fresh Parsley
- 1 Tbsp Chopped Fresh Dill
- 3 tbsp.
- Kosher salt and freshly ground black pepper

Salad:

- 1 cup barley
- 2 chicken cups chicken stock
- Zest and 1 lemon juice
- 1 tbsp wholegrain mustard
- 1 tablespoon dried parsley
- Extra cup extra-virgin vegetable oil
- Kosher salt and freshly ground black pepper
- 2 heads red -Pallet lettuce, chopped
- 1 purple onion, halved and thinly sliced
- 1-pint cherry tomatoes, chopped
- 2 avocados, chopped

Instructions

1. Lemon-green Chica's: Place chicken during a large reusable bag. During a medium bowl, mix vegetable oil, lemon rind, juice, parsley, dill, and parsley. Put the pickle in the bag, seal it, and refrigerate for half an hour.

2. Make a salad: Meanwhile, during a medium saucepan, bring barley and chicken stock to a boil over medium heat. When it comes to a boil, cover the pot and cook the barley until tender, 35 to 45 minutes: drain and reserve.

3. During a medium bowl, mix the lemon peel, juice, mustard, and parsley together. Gradually mix vegetable oil and whisk well—season with salt and pepper.

4. Prepare your grill for top heat. Remove chicken from pickle and season with salt and pepper.

5. Fry, the chicken until it is well stocked on both sides and fully cooked for 10 to 12 minutes. Remove chicken from grill and reserve.

6. During a large bowl, toss the lettuce, onion, and tomato together. Add dressing and toss well to coat.

7. Slice the chicken and serve over the salad with avocado.

Harissa Kabuli Gram Stew with Eggplant

Ingredients

2 servings

- 1 cup millet
- Kosher salt
- 2 tablespoons ghee (or any other neutral, high heat oil), divided
- 1 big Japanese eggplant
- Fresh black pepper,
- 1 onion chopped
- 3 garlic cloves, minced

- 2 large Campest harissa
- Drained, 1 bunch garnish of cilantro

Instructions

1. A medium saucepan with 2 cups of water as Do not fill out and millet and add a pinch of salt. Bring back to a boil, cover, reduce to a boil and cook for 25 minutes. Once the millet is cooked, remove the lid, inflate it with a fork and allow it to cool.

2. Meanwhile, heat 1 tbsp of ghee or oil during a deep-frying pan over medium heat. Add the season with the eggplant, salt, and pepper, and cook until tender and golden brown, adding more ghee for about 10 minutes to prevent the eggplant from the skeleton. Transfer the eggplant to a bowl and set it aside.

3. Pour remaining 1 tbsp of ghee or oil in an equal pan, add onion and cook for 8 to 10 minutes till it becomes soft and golden brown.

4. Add garlic and cook for two minutes. Season with salt and pepper, then add tomatoes, chickpeas, and herbs. Return the eggplant to the pan and reduce heat to low; Allow to boil for 10 to fifteen minutes.

5. Divide between two bowls and top with the stew. Garnish with a pair of cilantro leaves and serve hot.

Salad with Grilled Halloumi and Herbs

Ingredients

4 servings

- Half a lemon
- 1 pound tomato, chopped rounds
- Flaky salt and the latest ground pepper
- Extra virgin vegetable oil

- ½ pound halloumi cheese Hua, sliced in 4 slabs
- 5 basil leaves, torn
- 2 tablespoons finely Italian Parsley chopped

Instructions

1. Preheat a grill or grill pan over medium-high heat.

2. Arrange tomatoes on a serving platter or four plates. Squeeze the lemon lightly and add flaky salt and pepper over it.

3. Brush the grill grates with oil, then add turmeric and cook, turning once, until the scars appear, and so the cheese is heated for about 1 minute per side. Place it over the tomatoes. Drizzle the salad with vegetable oil and sprinkle with basil and parsley. Serve immediately.

Chapter 6: Mediterranean Diet Snack Recipes

Blueberry Coconut Energy Bits

Ingredients

- 1 cup old-fashioned oatmeal or gluten-free oats
- 1/4 cup ground flaxseed

- Seeds 2 tablespoons chia seeds
- 1/4 teaspoon ground cinnamon
- One pinch sea salt
- 1/2 cup creamy almond butter
- 1/4 cup honey
- 1/2 teaspoon vanilla
- 1/2 teaspoon coconut extracts optional
- 1/4 cup dried blueberries
- 1/4 cup sweetened flaked coconut combine

Instructions

- In a large bowl, oats, ground linseed, chia seeds, cinnamon, and salt.
- Keep the almond butter during a small microwave-safe bowl. Heat within the microwave for 20-30 seconds or until slightly melted. Stir until smooth.
- Mix honey, vanilla and coconut extracts in melted almond butter. Stir until smooth. Pour over oat mixture and stir until well combined. Stir within the dried blueberries and coconut.
- Roll the mixture into small balls, about 1-2 tablespoons per ball. Keep in an airtight container and refrigerate for 2 weeks. You will also keep the balls within the freezer for 1 month.

Mediterranean-Style Dip with Roasted Squash

Ingredients

- 1 Acorn Squash
- Private Reserve extra virgin vegetable oil
- 2 peeled, peel with and finely chopped
- 1 15-oz Cannellini beans, dried Artist Pun
- 1 sliced clove, chopped
- 3/4 teaspoon Spanish Paprika
- 3/4 coriander
- 3 / 4 tsp ground cumin seeds.
- 3/4 teaspoon ground sumac

- 1/2 teaspoon cayenne pepper, more if you like a spicy dip, garnish with
- 2 teaspoons fresh juice for
- Flat-leaf, celery,
- 2 teaspoons toasted pine garnish, nuts for
- 2 g toasted slivered almonds

Instructions

- Preheat the oven for 400 degrees f.
- Microwave squash and keep in warm on high for 3 minutes (this will make cutting through the skin harder easier).
- Carefully cut the sliced squash in half through the stem. And employing a spoon, scoop out the seeds. (You can discard the seeds, or clean or toast them to use as a garnish)
- Sprinkle the squash with salt, then place the meat side down on a lightly oiled baking sheet.
- Fry for 40 minutes in a 400-degree F-oven until the meat is tender and slightly brown around the edges.
- While the squash is roasting, prepare the caramelized shallots. During a wok, heat 1 tbsp of private reserve extra virgin vegetable oil on medium-high. Toss regularly, shallow, and sauté until caramelized—season with salt.
- When the squash is ready, remove from the oven and allow it to cool. Take out the meat and discard the shell.

- In an outdoor kitchen tool bowl fitted with a blade, add 1/2 quantity of shallots (remaining to garnish); Squash (meat only); White beans; All the spices; Sprinkling of salt. Add the juice and three tablespoons of private reserve extra virgin vegetable oil. Turn off the highest of your processor and blend until you achieve a smooth dip. Taste and adjust the salt or add more spices to your liking. Blend again.
- Transfer the dip to a serving bowl. Add vegetable oil, parsley leaves, and a drizzle of toasted nuts. Enjoy with hot Chita, Chita chips, or crackers!

Spring Peas + Fava Bean Guacamole with Root Chips

Ingredients

- 5 large root vegetables (you can use a golden or red beet mixture or turnip)
- Cajetan oil
- Salt for spring peas
- 20 English peas, peas away from pods,
- 6 fava beans, pods and Bean away from the outer skin.
- 4 ripe avocado nick acid
- 1/2 juice; one lemon 1/2 of

- One handful fistula, chopped
- Little purple onion (about 1/4 cup), finely
- Smoked paprika, a pinch of
- Salt and pepper
- A pinch Pepper Flakes (optional)

Instructions

- Preheat oven to 300°. Line an outer baking sheet with parchment paper.
- Cut the roots thin with a mandolin, but not a thin one, you will want them to possess a touch weight. Spread the sliced roots on a parchment-lined baking sheet. Brush them lightly with vegetable oil. Do not add salt anymore, and this will lengthen the water and make the chips thick.
- Place another piece of parchment on top of the roots, then lay another baking sheet on top. Once baked, it may help to keep the chips flat.
- Bake the chips for about 20 minutes. Pull them out and remove the baking sheet that is on top and put them back inside the oven for an additional 15-20 minutes. Keep an eye on them and flush out any substance that starts brown on the sides.
- When they are done, transfer the chips to a wire rack to cool. As they are going hard and crisp to cool.

- When they have cooled down, finish by seasoning them with salt.
- While the chips are cooling, serve guacamole +.
- Place a small pot of water on the stove and bring to a boil. Prepare an ice bath and prepare it next to boiling water.
- Place the peas and fava in boiling water and cook for 3-4 minutes. When the peas and fava beans are tender, remove the slated spoon and place it in an ice bath. After about 2 minutes, strain the peas and beans with an ice bath.
- Smash the avocado with a fork until it suits your desire. Add juice, cilantro, and purple onion smoked paprika, and stir to mix. Mix salt, pepper, and cayenne flakes to taste.
- Top with peas and fava beans and serve immediately with base chips.
- I recommend making guacamole fresh and do not keep it for too long because it will oxidize. However, chips are often made ahead of time and stored in an airtight container.

Beet Chips

Ingredients

- 6-8 medium-large beets
- Olive oil
- 1 tbsp flaked sea salt
- 1 tbsp dried chives

Instructions

- Trim the greens and so the roots. Rub the beets well under cold water but leave the skins on. Use a mandolin to thin the beats 1/16 ". If you do not have a mandolin, use a sharp knife to thin the beets.
- Preheat the oven to 400 degrees Fahrenheit. Drizzle a very fine amount of vegetable oil to the baking sheet pan, then rub the oil on top of the pan with your hands or a towel. You will like this as a very minimal crust, not only because the beets do not stick, but not so much that they cook within the oil, or they are going to steam instead of bake, and lime is available instead of being crisp. Be careful not to overlap, layer the sliced beets on the pan. You will need quite a sheet pan, and/or reuse the pan in batches of baking.
- Bake the chips on a rock bottom rack of the oven for 10–15 minutes, counting how thin the beets are and the way they are large.
- While the beets are baking, pour the salt in a small bowl and mix the dried chives into the salt. You will do that step ahead of time because the longer the herbs are within the salt, the more delicious the salt will be.
- Remove the rack from the oven and sprinkle with chive salt. Allow the beets to cool on the griddle; they will crisp as they cool. Once cooled, transfer to a cooling rack to still dry and crisp. Repeat with remaining slices of beets.

Greek Fried Zucchini

Ingredients

- 2 lbs. Zucchini (about 4 medium)
- Kosher salt
- 4 slices sliced (about I cup)
- 2 tablespoons freshly chopped dill

- 2 tablespoons freshly chopped parsley
- 1 tablespoon
- 1 album
- 2/3 Gigeta cheese
- ½ cup white whole dough
- ½ teaspoon Cheuk
- ¼ cup whole Wheat Breadcrumbs
- Black pepper
- 2 tablespoons Jupiter oil
- to serve Lemon

Tzatziki Nail:
- Half cup plain nonfat Greek yogurt
- 1/3 cup finely chopped or grated cucumber
- 1 clove garlic, minced
- 1 tablespoon juice
- 1 tablespoon freshly chopped dill

Instructions

- To make tzatziki, combine yogurt, cucumber, garlic, juice, and dill during a bowl. Refrigerate until able to use it.
- To make fritters grate with zucchini (on the skin) over a box grater. Grind the zucchini at an angle to insist on longer strands.

- Keep the grated zucchini with cheesecloth during a colander. If you do not have a cheesecloth, you will put the zucchini directly inside the colander. Sprinkle 2 tablespoons of salt over the zucchini and toss to mix.
- Allow the zucchini to rest for 20 minutes, then collect the ends of the cheesecloth and drain out all the liquid. If you are not using cheesecloth, you will squeeze the zucchini water together with your hands or use it in batches. It is possible to squeeze out as much of the water as possible so that the fritters are not soggy - you will be surprised at what proportion the water comes out!
- Put the zucchini in a large bowl and add the flakes, dill, parsley, egg, and albumen. Mix with a fork to mix.
- Add cheese, flour, yeast, breadcrumbs, one teaspoon salt, and teaspoon pepper. Mix all ingredients well with a fork.
- Heat 1 tbsp of vegetable oil over medium heat during a large forged iron pan or nonstick frypan. Put 8 dolls (about 2 tablespoons each) of the zucchini in the pan and flatten them slightly with a spatula. The more you level them, the crisper the fritters will be.
- Cook 3-4 minutes until a golden-brown crust is formed, then flip them over. Cook for another 2-3 minutes until it is again bottomed.
- Take out the fritters from the pan. Pour the remaining spoon oil in the pan and repeat the method with the remaining solution.

- Serve the fritters hot and garnish with fresh herbs and lemon wedges. Serve with Tzatziki or plain Greek yogurt.

Greek Spinach Artichoke Dip

Ingredients

- 1 10 oz Package Frozen Spinach, Melted
- 1 14 oz Artichoke Heart, Dried and Chopped
- 1 1/3 Cups Plain Greek Yogurt (Whole Milk, 2%, Nonfat All Work)

- 2 Cloves Garlic, Minced Hua (or 2 tsp) minced meat)
- 6 oz feta, broken (about 1 cup) cup of cup
- Chopped 2/3mozzarella, plus chopped 1/3more toppings
- parmesan.

Instructions

- Preheated oven to 350F 1-quart quart Dish or 8 × 8 glass pan, set aside.
- Ensure that the frozen spinach liquid is completely melted before squeezing out. To squeeze out the liquid, I cut a small hole within the bag and squeezed the spinach within the bag and let the water out. Then I opened the bag completely and pressed the towel into the spinach to take in more water. You will also use cheesecloth. Transfer the spinach to a medium bowl,
- Add within the remainder of your ingredients, the sliced artichoke begins with hearts, ending with Greek yogurt and sliced Parmesan. Fold the ingredients together with a large spatula to mix, mixing well together.
- Transfer mixture to prepared baking dish, topping with mozzarella and more sprinkles of Parmesan.
- Bake for 25-30 minutes, until the cheese topping turns golden. You will turn off the oven in the last 5 minutes to make the cheese golden.

- Serve with your favorite chips, crackers, and/or vegetables, enjoy!

7-Ingredient Quinoa Granola

Ingredients

- 1 cup Bob's Red Mill Old-Old Oatmeal (gluten-free for GF eaters)
- 1/2 cup Uncovered Bob's Red Mill White Quota
- 2 cups raw almonds (roughly chopped)

- 1 tbsp coconut sugar (or sub-organic sugar, muscovado, or organic sugarcane)
- 1 pinch sea salt
- 3 1/2 tablespoons copra oil
- 1/4 cup syrup (or agave nectar)

Instructions

- Preheat oven to 340 degrees F (171 C) But When reheated.
- In a bowl, add oats, quinoa, almonds, coconut sugar, and salt - stir to mix.
- In a little saucepan, add copra oil and syrup. Heat over medium heat for 2-3 minutes, repeatedly whisking until the 2 are fully combined and until there is a separate separation.
- Immediately pour over the dry ingredients and shake all oats and nuts to mix until well coated. Arrange on an outer baking sheet and spread in a fine layer.
- Bake for 20 minutes. Then remove from the oven and shake/toss granola. Turn the pan around, so the other end goes into the oven first (so it bakes evenly) and bake 5-10 minutes more. Watch carefully, not burning. You would know that this is done when the granola is dark golden brown and is fragrant.
- Allow cooling completely before enjoying it. Store leftovers during temperature in a sealed bag or container for two weeks or within the freezer for 1 month.

Mediterranean Roasted Gram

Ingredients

- 215 15 oz Chick
- 2 tsp Extra Virgin Vegetable Oil
- 2 tsp Wine Vinegar

- 2 tsp Fresh Juice
- 1 tsp Kosher Salt
- 1 tsp Dry Parsley
- 1/2 tsp Garlic Powder
- 1/2 tsp Black Pepper

Instructions

- 425 ovens from preheating the oven. Degree and line up a baking sheet with parchment paper. Let the chickpeas dry, rinse and dry well, then lay on the baking sheet during a crust.
- Fry for 10 minutes, then remove from the oven, use a spatula to show the chickpeas, so they bake evenly, then fry for an additional 10 minutes.
- In a large bowl, combine the remaining ingredients and whisk. Add the recent chickpeas and toss gently until completely coated.
- Place the coated chickpeas on a baking sheet and continue frying for 10 more minutes, occasionally making sure to check that they do not overcook and burn. Allow yourself to chill and enjoy fully!

Smoked Eggplant Dip: Baba Ganesh

Ingredients

- 1 Eggplant
- 2 Tbsp Tahini Paste
- 1 1/2 teaspoon Greek Yogurt
- 1 Clove, chopped
- 1 tsp juice
- Salt & Pepper
- 1, for Garnish
- 3/4 Tsp Aleppo Chili
- 1 / Tsp crushed. Red Chili (optional)

- Toasted Pine Garnish
- Salad Topping for
- 1 Tomato Pal, Chopped,
- 1/2 English Cucumber Chopped
- Parsley Large Fist Fresh
- Salt and Black Pepper
- 1/2 Spoon Sumac
- Splash Fresh Juice
- Extra Virgin Vegetable Oil Drizzle Early Harvest

Instruction.

- Salad Upper Layer. Add tomatoes, cucumber, and parsley during a bowl—season with salt, pepper, and sums. Add extra virgin vegetable oil juice and a generous drizzle. Toss and keep aside.
- Smoke Eggplant: Turn on 1 gas jet on high. Employing a pair of tongs, rotate the eggplant approximately every 5 minutes until the eggplant is completely soft and the skin is crooked around it (about 15 to twenty minutes.) Don't worry. If the eggplant is deflected, it is perceived. (You can also do this on a gas or charcoal grill at medium-high heat.) Remove from heat and allow the eggplant to cool.
- Eggplant skin and drain Remove excess water. Once the eggplants are cool enough to touch, peel off the crispy skin.

Discard the stem. Transfer eggplant meat to a colander; Leave it for 3 minutes.

- Take a dive—transfer eggplant meat to a kitchen appliance bowl. Add tahini paste, yogurt, garlic, juice, salt, pepper, sumac, Aleppo pepper, crushed red (if using) just provides some pulses to mix (do not over mix. See note)) To.
- Smoked eggplant dip to a serving bowl. Cover and refrigerate for half an hour (or overnight).
- Bring eggplant dip to temperature. Top with a generous drizzle of extra virgin vegetable oil. Add pine nuts. Spoon the salad over the top (bound to drain off any excess liquid before adding to the top of the Baba Ganesh.) Serve with hotly beaten wedges or beaten chips.

Note: Allow half an hour of idle time for the dip to rest.

Pro-tip: You are trying to dip a chunky, rustic eggplant here. Avoid over-blending with kitchen equipment, or it will overflow. You do not need to use kitchen equipment to dip Baba Ganesh. If you are afraid to over-blend it and make it too movable, avoid using kitchen tools. Instead, use a bowl and a fork to easily melt the eggplant and mix the rest of the ingredients as remaining.

Make-Ahead Tip: You will prepare eggplant dip (Baba Ganesh) ahead of time (steps 2 to 5). Refrigerate during a tight-lid glass container (without salad toppings). Baba Ganesh will be fine for three days. Bring it to temperature, topping Evo, pine nuts, and, therefore, salad toppings. You will prepare the topping of the salad 1 night in advance, and make sure to refrigerate it in your separate container. Drain excess water before use.

Pro-tip: If you favor, you will serve the salad instead and allow guests to serve with a spoon whatever the amount of the salad during their dip.

Oven-Roasted Option: If you do not have the means to cook the eggplant on an open flame, you will roast the eggplant within the oven. Follow this easy baba ghanoush recipe for instruction.

Crock Pot Chunky Monkey Paleo Trail Mix

Ingredients

- 2 cups raw walnuts (halved or chopped)
- 1 cup raw cashew nuts or whole almonds also work)
- 1 cup coconut flakes (be bound to be chopped)
- 1/3 cup coconut sugar
- 1 to 1.5 Tbsp in butter (chopped) slices) or room tempo 2 to 3 tablespoons of copra oil too unripe
- Extract 1 teaspoon vanilla or butter
- 6 ounces banana chips or slices of dried banana

- 1/2 cup to 2/3 cup Bitter watch Chocolate Chips or Paleo Feud Chunks (we use) Enjoy Life Foods brand)

Instructions

- Put your nuts, coconut, sugar, vanilla and butter slices or copra oil in a crockpot. Mix and keep on high for 45-hours. Make sure not to burn coconut flakes. Note- Reduce after 45 minutes if the flakes are cooking fast or brown.
- Turn on low and continue cooking for 20-30 minutes.
- Remove and place the crockpot material on parchment paper to take out. Allow it to cool for at least one and a half hours before adding chocolate and banana chips.
- Add banana chips and chocolate chips within and mix.
- The alternative - cooking banana chips - you will add to your unsweetened banana chips to cook with nuts/coconut, instead of adding water. But you will have to shake often and cook for only 45 minutes.
- An airtight container or store in Ziplock bags
- See notes to lighter Sunstroke

Greek Guacamole

Ingredients

- Have 2 large ripe avocados (halves, pit removed)
- 2 tbsp juice
- 1 heaping tbsp dried tomatoes sun sliced
- Cooked 3 slices
- 1/4 onion
- 1 dried parsley (or sub-fresh)
- Chopped 2 tablespoons freshly chopped parsley
- 4 tablespoons whole kalamata olives (sliced and chopped // optional)

- 1 pinch each sea salt and pepper

Instructions

- Add avocado and juice to an outside bowl and use a potato masher, pastry cutter, or large fork to mash and mix.
- Add remaining ingredients (olives are optional) and shake to mix. Take a sample of salt and pepper and pour it if necessary.
- Adjust other flavors if necessary, adding more lemons for acidity, sun-dried tomatoes for deeper tomato flavor, onion for crunch/spice, or parsley or oregano.
- Enjoy immediately with Chita, Chita Chips or Vegetables! Best when fresh, although leftover refrigerators limit to 2-3 days.

Roasted Veggie Chips

Ingredients

4/6 servings

- 4 small golden beets
- 4 small red beets
- 2 small turnips

- 2 medium parsnips
- 1 bunch radish
- 3 tablespoons extra virgin vegetable oil
- 1½ tablespoons salt
- 2 tablespoons freshly ground black pepper
- 3 tablespoons chopped fresh Herbs (egg rosemary), sage, and/or thyme)

Instructions

- Preheat the oven at 400 ° F. Line two baking sheets with parchment paper.
- Cut the vegetables approximately (inch thick (as thin as possible). Employing the slicing side of a mandolin or a box grater can speed up the method, but a knife also works.
- Vegetables Toss the veggies in a bowl with the oil (you want to toss the red beets separately to avoid turning everything pink). Spread them in a fine layer on the prepared baking sheet, making sure. They are not overlapping.
- Sprinkle salt, pepper, and herbs evenly on 2 baking sheets. Fry the vegetables for 20 to 25 minutes, until golden brown and crisp. Serve. First, cool completely. At the very least, store in an airtight container to keep in mind the crunchy texture to a week.

Homemade Taj Tiki-Style Sauce

Ingredients

- 1 1/2 C plain Greek Dh or Campion Schor (or you'll change it with dairy-free alternatives, such as almonds, cashews, soybeans, yogurt made, etc.)
- 3/4 c fresh cucumber, deciding (Force dice into very small pieces)
- 1 1/2 teaspoons dill (I usually use dried dill weed)

- 1 tbsp garlic powder
- 1/4 tsp ground black pepper
- 1/4 tsp salt

Instructions

Combine all ingredients during a bowl and serve chilled. How easy?! Serve with veggie, crackers, beaten or use as a topper for grilled chicken, fish, meat - or anything else!

Note: This dip is best served immediately, as cucumbers can make the dip watery if left out for too long. If you are making this dip ahead of time, allow the cucumbers to empty on the towel for a few hours inside the fridge so that they do not hold the maximum amount of water (you can place a container with the towel, Place cucumber on top and canopy with lid). This dip stays inside the fridge for about 3 days, but if entertaining, it is best to prepare it before serving.

Greek Hummus Pita Cutting

Ingredients

- 4 7-inch pita bread, digging 4 pita triangles {of 16 triangles
- 3/4 cup Sabra roasted red pepper Hummus
- 1/2 cup cracked feta cheese
- 1-pint cherry tomato,} chopped,
- peeled 1/2 large, Seeds removed and kalamata
- sliced, chopped 10olives, chopped
- 1/2 cup pepperoncini peppers.
- 1 teaspoon extra virgin vegetable oil
- 1/2 teaspoon dried oregano

Instructions

- 16 cut pita bread into triangles and arrange on an outsized plate or baking sheet
- Spread a thin layer of roasted red chili hummus on one side of each pieta triangle.
- In a medium bowl, combine tomato, feta cheese, cucumber, olives, pepperoncini, extra virgin vegetable oil, and parsley.
- Top each Peeta Triangle with the Greek Salad mixture.
- Serve immediately or refrigerate in an airtight container.
- These are best served immediately. If you want to make them ahead, I can wait to keep the Greek salad mixture until you are able to serve as the juice can start to form as beaten bread.

Rainbow Heirloom Tomato Bruschetta

Ingredients

8 servings

- 1 baguette, finely chopped and toasted
- 3 garlic cloves,
- 16 ounces whole milk ricotta cheese
- Kosher salt and freshly ground black pepper
- ¼ cup basil pesto
- 2 tablespoons vegetable oil

- 2 tablespoons vinegar
- 2 tablespoons sauce.
- 1 red tomato, half and thinly sliced
- 1 yellow tomato, half and thinly sliced
- 1 green tomato, half and thinly sliced
- 1 pint of heirloom cherry tomatoes chopped fresh basil leaves.

Instructions

1 to serve. Rub the surface of each baguette slice with garlic sauce. The season of ricotta with salt and pepper was then spread on baguette slices.

2. During a medium bowl, whisk together pesto, olive oil, balsamic vinegar, and dill. Add tomatoes and toss gently.

3. Working in color blocks, arranging tomatoes on baguette slices; Season with salt and pepper. Top with basil leaves.

Chapter 7: Mediterranean Diet Dinner Recipes

One-Pot Greek Chicken and Lemon Rice

Ingredients

- 5 Chicken Thighs, On Skin, Bone (about 1 kg / 2 lb.) (Note 1)
- 1 - 2 Lemons, Zest + 4 Tbsp Juice (Note 7) of
- 1 Tbsp. Use dried oregano

- 4 garlic cloves, minced
- 1/2 tsp salt
- Rice
- 1 1/2 tsp vegetable oil, separated
- 1 small onion,
- 1 cup / 180 g long grain rice (note 6 for other rice)
- 1 1/2 cup / 375 ml chicken stock / stock
- 3/4 cup/water
- 1 tbsp today Ayn leaf
- 3/4 Salt
- Pepper
- 185 Multipin garnish
- Finely chopped parsley or oregano (optional)
- Fresh lemon rind (highly recommended)

Instructions

- Mix chicken and marinade ingredients during a Ziplock bag. Keep aside for at least 20 minutes but overnight.
- Cook for.
- Preheat 180C / 350F oven
- Remove the chicken from the marinade but reserve the marinade.
- Heat 1/2 tbsp of vegetable oil over medium-high heat during a deep, heavy-based pan (Note 2).

- Place the chicken inside the skillet, down the skin side, and cook until golden brown, then flip and cook upside down until golden brown. Remove the chicken and keep it aside.
- Pour off the fat and wipe the pan with a scrubbed ball or towel (to remove the black bits), then return to the stove.
- Heat 1 tbsp of vegetable oil inside the pan over medium-high heat. Add onion and sauce for a minute or two until translucent. Then add the remaining Rice ingredients and reserved marinade.
- Allow the liquid to come to a boil and let it boil for 30 seconds. Place the chicken on top, then place a lid on the skillet (note 3)—Bake within the oven for 35 minutes. Then remove the lid and bake for an additional 10 minutes, or until all the liquid is absorbed and so the rice is tender (hence a total of 45 minutes).
- Remove from the oven and allow to rest for five to 10 minutes before serving, garnish with parsley or oregano and fresh lemon peel, if desired.

Recipe Note:

1. I exploit bone thighs, skin-on chicken thighs because there is more flavor. But if you favor, you will use smooth, smooth, smooth thigh straps. If you are doing this, place the chicken in the pan within 20 minutes at a baking time as the chicken will not be needed for long.

For drumsticks, you won't be ready to find them as successfully, but that's fine, just briefly compress and bake for the entire time (45 minutes).

It can also be made with the breast, but it will not be as juicy as the meat is not juicy.

2. The fry pan I used was 26cm / 10 "diameter and 6cm / 2.4" deep. This is the perfect size for this.

3. I don't have a lid for the frying pan I use, but I also have a lid for a large pot that I just put on top. Otherwise, the foil works fine, or perhaps a baking tray.

4. I garnished it with slices of lemon, which I discovered within the pan after cooking the chicken.

5. The way to make it perfectly on the stovetop (readers' request): Although the result is not the same as baking because you either mix chicken juice with rice or crispy skin, it is often made entirely. Is. on the stove. There are two options:

a) Cook the chicken completely on the stove, keep aside, and cook the rice on the stove (reduce the liquid by 1/2 cup). To cook rice, just follow the instructions in the recipes until the purpose before putting them in the oven. Instead of doing this, keep the lid on medium and cook on medium-low until the liquid is absorbed (about 12 - 15 minutes). When the rice is almost ready, pop the chicken back on top of the rice and put the lid on to warm, and finish cooking the rice. It can produce crispy-skinned chicken compared to the other method.

b) The second method is to find the chicken but not through cooking it, then pop the rice on top of the rice to cook. This method is simple, and you will get the benefit of mixing chicken juice with rice while cooking, but you will lose the dryness of the skin.

What I can suggest is using skinless, boneless thigh fillets instead, in such a way that you don't have to worry about skin dryness, but you get all the flavors!

6. This recipe will work with white long-grain, medium, and short-grain rice, but I prefer to recommend long-grain as it is the smallest amount among the three types. It will also work with jasmine, normal rice, wild rice, and normal basmati rice. Rice will be covered in quarter-hour for about 1 hour, open 10 minutes, so the chicken is going to be super tender. I do not recommend brown basmati rice as it takes longer to cook. Risotto and paella rice are also not recommended - the liquid absorption level varies greatly, making the recipe an excessive amount of change.

7. You would like enough lemons to urge four lemon juice, which can be 1 big or 2 small lemons. Use all the zest from lemons you just use.

8. NO MARJORAM: Very few readers have inquired about this. If you found this recipe through Pinterest, you will notice that

there is an anomaly within the ingredients showing marjoram within the ingredients. This recipe was once marjoram! Please use the recipe as it is written.

9. Nutrition per serving (5 servings) This assumes that it is often made using trimmed bone, skin-on chicken thigh straps. This does not consider the fat coming out of the pan after searing the chicken, which suggests that they are calories per serving.

Pan Mediterranean Cod

Ingredients

- 2 tablespoons vegetable oil doll
- 1 small onion chopped
- 2 cups chopped fennel
- 3 large cloves garlic chopped

- 1 14.5 oz tomatoes can be
- 1 cup of fresh tomatoes.
- 2 cups chopped Kelpie Spoon ripe
- 1/2 cup water
- Pouchful of red chili
- 2 fresh oregano or 1/2 tsp dried oregano
- 1 cup oil black olive
- 1 lb. Cod Digging 4 Parts
- 1/8 Salt
- 1/4 Black Pepper
- 1/4 Fennel Seeds Optional
- 1 Orange Peel.
- Fresh Oregano Fennel, Orange, Olive Oil

Instructions

- Over medium heat in a large pan (ideally with high sides), 8 Eat onion, fennel, and garlic in vegetable oil for minutes, season with salt and pepper (about 1/4 teaspoon of each). Add canned diced tomatoes, fresh tomatoes, bananas, and water. Stir well and cook for 12 minutes. Add crushed red chili, fresh oregano, and olives.
- Prepare season with fish, salt, pepper, orange peel, and fennel seeds (optional). Keel tomato stew mix in Nestle fish. Cover the pan and cook for 10 minutes.

- Remove from heat and finish with fennel fronts on top, more fresh parsley, more orange peel, and a drizzle of vegetable oil.
- Serve immediately.

Mediterranean Couscous with Chicken Souvlaki Kebab

Ingredients

- Chicken Souvlaki Kabobs
- 1-pound skinless, boneless pigeon breast halves, digging 1/2-inch strips

- 1 cup chopped fennel (reserved leaves, if necessary)
- ⅓ cup dry wine
- ¼ cup juice
- 3 tablespoons vegetable oil
- 4 Lung Lashaun, minced
- 2 teaspoons dried oregano, crushed
- ½ teaspoon salt
- ¼ teaspoon pepper
- Lemon wedges
- Mediterranean couscous
- 1 tablespoon vegetable oil
- ½ cup Israeli (large pearl) couscous
- 1 cup form Ni
- ½ cup snipped dried (not oil-packed)
- ¾ cup chopped red sweet pepper
- Chi cup chopped cucumber
- Tomatoes topped cup chopped red onion
- Fat cup plain Fat-free Greek yogurt
- Ed cups finely chopped fresh basil leaves
- Sun cup peeled fresh parsley
- 1 tbsp juice
- East spoon salt
- ¼ teaspoon pepper

Instructions

Step 1. Kabobs: Place the chicken and chopped fennel during a shallow dish set in a resealable bag. For marinade, mix wine, juice, oil, garlic, parsley, salt, and pepper during a small bowl. Remove 1/4 cup of marinade and keep aside.

Step 2 Add the remaining pickles to the chicken mixture. Seal bag; Address coat chicken mixture. Marinate the refrigerator within 1 1/2 hours, rotating the bag once

Step 3. Meanwhile, while using wooden skewers, soak eight 10- to 12-inch skewers in half the water. Discard dry chicken, pickles, and fennel. Thread chicken, accordion-style, on the dagger.

Step 4. Grill Chicken Skewer, covered, in medium-high heat 6 to eight minutes or until the chicken is once pink. Remove from grill and brush with reserved 1/4 cup marinade.

Step 5. Prepare couscous: 1 teaspoon vegetable oil over medium heat during a small saucepan heat. Add 1/2 cup Israeli couscous (large pearls). Cook 4 minutes or until brown and shake. Add 1 cup of water. Come back to boiling, warm down. Simmer, covered, 10 minutes or until the cousin is tender and the liquid is absorbed, adding 1/2 cup of snipped dried tomatoes (not filled with oil) over the final 5 minutes; Cold. Transfer couscous to a bowl. 3/4 cup chopped red sweet peppers, 1/2 cup each chopped cucumber and chopped purple onion, 1/3 cup plain fat-free Greek yogurt, 1/4 cup each finely chopped fresh basil leaves and peeled fresh Parsley, 1 cup. Spoon juice and 1/4 teaspoon each salt and pepper.

Step 6. Serve Kebabs with couscous, lemon wedges, and fennel leaves if desired.

Garlic Swiss Chard & Chickpea Shed Swiss Chard

Ingredients

- 1 tbsp Vegetable Oil Bite
- 2 Center stems are cut apart and
- 2 cups low sodium chicken stock or vegetable broth
- 2 medium peeled chopped (about 1/2 cup) 6 medium Garlic is discarded. Cloves, minced chopped

- 15.5 oz chickpeas, chickpeas and garbanzo beans with
- 2 tablespoons freshly squeezed juice
- salt and freshly ground black pepper for taste.
- 1/2 cup feta cheese. Optional

Instructions

- It can be heated, in a large pan, over medium heat 1 tbsp of more vegetable oil—high temperature. Add half the seeds and cook for 1 to 2 minutes. When the primary half has dried, add the remaining four. When all the chutney has been wiped, add the chicken stock. Cover the skillet and cook for about 10 minutes until tender. Dry the chard through a sieve and set it aside.
- Wipe the skillet and heat the remaining 1 tbsp of vegetable oil over medium-high heat. Simmer and garlic and cook until they are soft, about 2 minutes. Add the chat and chickpeas and cook for 3 to 4 minutes until it is hot. Squeeze the juice over the mixture and season with salt and pepper to taste. If desired, sprinkle cheese on top before serving.

Spinach Feta Grilled Cheese

Ingredients

- 1/2 teaspoon vegetable oil
- 1 clove garlic
- 1/4 frozen cut spinach powder
- Salt and pepper pinches
- 2 ciabatta rolls
- 1 cup mozzarella sugar Carta
- 1 oz feta cheese
- Pinch red chili flakes (optional)

Instructions

- Garlic mince and vegetable oil Add it to a pan. Cook on medium-low heat for 1-2 minutes, or until it begins to melt. Add the frozen spinach, reduce the heat to medium, and cook for about 5 minutes, or until it is hot and most of the surplus moisture has gone away. Season lightly with salt and pepper.
- Cut the rolls in half. Add about 1/4 cup of chopped mozzarella and 1/2 ounce. To rock each roll in half down. Divide the cooked spinach in between 2 sandwiches, then with a pinch of red chili flakes, 1/4 more sliced mozzarella on each.
- Place the highest half ciabatta rolls on the sandwich and transfer them to an outer non-stick pan. Fill an outer pot with a couple of inches of water to make the vat, then place the pot on top of the sandwich to press them like a penny press. Turn the heat to medium-low and cook until the sandwich is crispy on the bottom. Flip the sandwich carefully, put the weighted pot back up, and cook until it turns crisp on the opposite side, and so the cheese has melted. Serve hot

Mediterranean Chicken and Barley Salad

Ingredients

- ½ cup barley or barley mixture
- 1 water cup of water
- For a pinch of salt
- Salad
- 2 ripe skinless, odorless chicken breasts, sliced
- 3 mini cucumbers, diced
- 2 tomatoes, seeds and diced
- 5 sundried tomatoes, rehydrated and minced
- 3 tablespoons low-fat feta cheese, crumbled

- One small spoon
- 1 tbsp lemon peel
- 1/2 lemon juice
- 2 tablespoons vegetable oil
- Pepper Spoon Red Chili Flakes
- 3 tablespoons sunflower seeds
- 2 tablespoons peppermint, chiffonade

Instructions

Step 1. Put the spelling mixture of barley, water, and a pinch of salt during a small saucepan. Bring back to a boil, then reduce the heat to medium-low and boil for a quarter of an hour until the water is absorbed. Remove from warmth and funky.

Step 2 In a large bowl, cooled grains, chicken, cucumber, tomatoes, sun-dried tomatoes, feta, sumac, jest, juice, oil, red pepper flakes, sunflower seeds, peppermint, and a pinch. Merge together salts to taste.

Chestnut-Henna Crusted Salmon

Ingredients

- 2 teaspoons Dijon mustard
- 1 clove garlic, minced
- ¼ teaspoon lemon peel
- 1 teaspoon juice
- 1 teaspoon chopped fresh henna
- ½ teaspoon honey
- ½ teaspoon kosher salt
- ¼ teaspoon crushed red pepper
- 3 tablespoons Panko breadcrumbs
- 3 Tablespoons finely chopped walnuts
- 1 tablespoon extra-virgin vegetable oil
- 1 (1 pound) skinless salmon fillet, fresh or frozen

- Olive oil cooking spray
- Chopped fresh Lemon wedges for parsley and garnish

Instructions

Step 1: Preheat oven to an external Rimmed baking sheet lined with parchment paper to 425 ° F.

Step 2: In a small bowl, mix mustard, garlic, lemon peel, juice, rosemary, honey, salt, and crushed red chili. In another small bowl, mix the poncho, walnuts, and oil.

Step 3: Place the salmon on the prepared baking sheet. Spread the mustard mixture on top of the fish and, while pressing for the stick, sprinkle with the Panko mixture. Lightly coat with cooking spray.

Step 4: Bake until the fish flies easily with a fork, about 8 to 12 minutes, counting on the thickness.

Step 5: Sprinkle with parsley and, if desired, serve with lemon juice.

Sun-Dried Tomato and Feta Seth Couscous

Ingredients

- 1/3 cup Shell pine nuts
- 1 tbsp vegetable oil
- 1/2 teaspoon cocoa salt
- 1 1/2 cups couscous
- 1/3 cup sun-dried tomatoes, drained and
- Crumbled 1/3 cup feta cheese
- 1/4 cup chopped

Instructions

- In a dry, non-stick Tawa pan over medium-high heat, toast the pine nuts, often tossing, until golden brown, about 3-4 minutes. Be sure to inspect them closely as they will burn quickly once heated.
- In a medium saucepan, bring 1 1/4 cups of water to a boil. Couscous stir within vegetable oil and kosher salt, cover, and take away from heat. Represent 5 minutes.
- Fluff couscous with a fork and stir within sun-dried tomatoes, feta cheese, chopped broth, and pine nuts. This dish is often served hot or at temperature.

Quinoa Tabbouleh

Ingredients

- 1 cup quinoa (170 grams)
- 2 cups water (500 grams)
- ½ cup chopped onion (50 grams)
- 1⅓ cup chopped tomatoes (240 grams)

- 1 cup finely chopped fresh mint (26 grams)
- ½ cup finely chopped Hua Parsley (30 g)
- Juice of one lemon
- Extra virgin vegetable oil to taste (optional)

Instructions

- Rinse quinoa with cold water.
- Boil water during a saucepan, add quinoa and boil for about a quarter of an hour or until all the water is absorbed. You will urge a more intense flavor by adding other ingredients (dried herbs, sea salt, tamarind or soy, juice, or apple cider vinegar) to the boiling water.
- Allow the quinoa to cool to temperature or add cold water. It should cool completely before making the salad.
- In a large bowl, place the quinoa and, therefore, the remaining ingredients. Add the juice and so extra virgin vegetable oil (optional) and stir.

Vegetable Soup

Ingredients

- 2 tablespoons vegetable oil
- 1 small onion, diced
- 2 large carrots, peeled and chopped
- 5 cloves garlic, minced
- 2 tablespoons cumin
- 1/2 teaspoon dried thyme
- 2 (15 oz) can fire-roasted tomatoes
- 1 (15 oz) can make chickpeas., dried and rinsed
- 1 cup of green lentils

- (1 quart) box Progresso vegetable cooking stock
- 3 cups of water
- 1 teaspoon salt
- 1 teaspoon pepper
- 1/2 teaspoon red pepper flakes
- 2 cups cabbage, removed and sliced ribs

Instructions

- A Heat vegetable oil on medium heat during large stock. Add onions and carrots, frequently stirring, until onions become tender and translucent.
- Add garlic, cumin, and parsley. Cook until fragrant. Add fire-roasted tomatoes and chickpeas.
- Add the lentils, then in the Progresso Vegetable Cooking Stock and water. Season with salt, pepper, and cayenne flakes. Bring soup to a boil, then turn right down to a light boil. Cook for half an hour, until the lentils turn soft.
- Transfer 3 cups of soup to a blender or kitchen appliance (force it to get a good mixture of veggie and broth). Puree mixture until smooth. Put pureed soup back into the pot and add bananas. Cook until cooked.

Crotch Pot Chicken Thighs with Artichokes and Sun-Dried Tomatoes

Ingredients

- 6 to 8 boneless, skinless chicken thighs
- Salt and freshly ground black pepper, to taste
- 1/2 teaspoon sweetened or smoked paprika
- 1/2 tbsp dry parsley

- 1 jar (14.75-ounces) grilled artichoke heart, 1, or 3-cup liquid preserved
- 4 cloves garlic, minced
- 1/3 cup artichoke heart liquid
- 1 bag (3.5-ounce) julienne-cut sun-dried tomato
- 3 tablespoons chopped fresh parsley

Instructions

- Spray with a 6-quart cart pot / slow cooking spray.
- Season chicken thighs with salt, pepper, paprika, and dried parsley; Grow the slow cooker in one layer.
- Add artichoke hearts to the chicken, Sprinkle with garlic.
- Take 1/3-cup of the liquid from the jar with the artichoke heart and pour it at the highest.
- The cover; Cook on high for 4 to 4-1/2 hours or for at least 6 hours.
- Add sun-dried tomatoes half an hour before cooking; Cover and still cook.
- Remove the cover on top of the cooking time.
- Sprinkle with fresh parsley and serve.

Roasted Herbs Salmon

Ingredients

- 4-ounce salmon fillets, about 1 1/2 inches thick
- 2 tablespoons Dijon mustard
- 2 tablespoons fresh juice

- 1 tablespoon fresh thyme (or 1 teaspoon dried)
- 1 tbsp minced fresh henna (or 1 teaspoon dried)
- 1 teaspoon dried parsley
- One Spoon Salt
- Black spoon ground black pepper
- Cooking spray
- 1 small yellow onion, thin
- 2 Tomato, Thin-Thin-String

Instructions

Step 1: Make three to 2-inch-long, 1/4-inch deep, evenly spaced slits with the highest of each salmon fillet.

Step 2: In a shallow dish, mix mustard, juice, thyme, rosemary, parsley, salt and pepper together. Add salmon and switch to coat each side. Cover with coverings and refrigerate for a quarter of an hour. (If you are employing an entire fish, do an equal amount of work. The marinade will perish in slits.) Reserve marinade.

Step 3: Preheat oven to 450 ° F. Coat the shallow baking pan with cooking spray. Arrange slices of onion and tomato in the bottom of the prepared pan. Place salmon on top of onions and tomatoes. Add the remaining pickle over the salmon. Roast 10 to fifteen minutes, until the fish is fork-tender.

Greek Quesadillas

Ingredients

- 8 (8 inches) flour tortillas
- 1 (10 oz) packages frozen chopped spinach, thawed and dried,
- 1/2 cup julienned sun-dried tomatoes in vegetable oil drained
- 1/2 cup chopped pitted kalamata olives
- 1 cup chopped mozzarella cheese
- 1 Kpc High
- 1tbsp fresh dill was crumbled Feralia Tighe Tikyani sauce
- 1 cup plain Greek yogurt
- 1 English cucumber, chopped
- 2 cloves garlic,

- 1 tablespoon chopped fresh dill
- 1 squeezed tbsp fresh juice
- 1 teaspoon Nonwind Chalke Nimbus
- 1 teaspoon land., Optional
- kosher salt and freshly ground black pepper, taste to taste
- 2 tablespoons vegetable oil:

Instructions

- To make Tzatziki sauce, mix Greek yogurt, cucumber, garlic, dill, juice, lemon peel, and mint during a small bowl, Season with salt and pepper to taste. Drizzle with vegetable oil. Refrigerate for at least 10 minutes, causing the flavor to melt; put aside.
- Preheat oven to 400 ° F. Line a baking sheet with parchment paper.
- Top tortillas with spinach, sun-dried tomatoes, olives, and cheese, then top with another tortilla. Make 4 quesadillas with the remaining tortillas.
- Place the quesadillas on the prepared baking sheet. Place in the oven and bake for about 8-10 minutes until the cheese melts.
- If desired, serve immediately with garnished tzatziki sauce with dill.

Chicken Piccata

Ingredients

- 1 Lemon
- 1 1/2 pounds boneless, skinless chicken breasts
- 1 teaspoon kosher salt
- 1 teaspoon freshly ground black pepper

- 1/3 cup all-purpose flour
- 3 tablespoons butter divided
- 2 tablespoons vegetable oil
- 1 cup chicken stock or wine, or both mix
- 2 tablespoons Capers Sakha and rotten

Instructions

- Slice lemon in half, one half of the juice, then slice in contrast cut in half to 1/8 "slices and put aside it. And half
- Chick Trim any excess fat from the breasts. Season each side of the chicken breasts evenly with kosher salt and freshly ground and dunk each breast in pepper, flour, shaking off any excess.
- Medium-over a high heat During the large bowl, add 2 tablespoons butter with vegetable oil. Add 4 pieces. Cook the chicken for 2-3 minutes more. A plate or sheet pan with foil and Move Nadwi. Continue with the remaining chicken.
- Reduce heat to medium, and chicken stock or wine (or add 1/2 cup. Two) juice, sliced lemon, and so scrape the broken bits on capers, pan Cook for 2-3 minutes.
- Stir within the remaining 1 teaspoon of butter until melted. Taste for seasoning and add sauce over chicken breasts. Serve with mashed potatoes or cabbage, polenta, or noodles.

Sweet Potato Noodles

Ingredients

4 servings

Almond Sauce:

- 2 tablespoons extra virgin vegetable oil
- 3 shallots, minced
- 2 garlic cloves, minced

- 3 tablespoons all-purpose flour
- 2 cups plain, sweet almond milk
- 2 tablespoons Dijon mustard
- Salt and freshly ground black pepper

Sweet Potato Noodles:
- 2 tablespoons Extra-Virgin Vegetable Oil
- 3 Sweet Potatoes, dig noodles (made from a spiralizer at work) to
- 4 cups roughly. Blue-black
- Salt and fresh ground pepper
- Cup toasted, salted almonds, roughly chopped

Instructions

- Russ. While a medium pot, heat vegetable oil over medium heat. For about 1 minute, add mustard and garlic and let it smell.
- Stir within the flour and cook, stirring continuously, for 1 minute. Add almond milk continuously to prevent lumps from forming within the sauce. Over medium heat until the mixture involves a boil. Simmer for 4 to five minutes.

- Whisk within Dijon mustard and sauce with salt and pepper. While preparing the noodles, cover the sauce on low heat and still heat it.
- Make Swill Potato Noodles: In a large saucepan, heat vegetable oil over medium heat. Add the sweet potato noodles and sauté, occasionally, until they are almost tender 5 to six minutes.
- Add bananas and toss until it is shaken. Add sauce and toss until the noodles are well coated.
- Before serving, toss to mix almonds and—season with salt and pepper. Serve immediately.

Mediterranean Baked Sadist Potato Sweet Potatoes

Ingredients

- 1/2 teaspoon vegetable oil
- 1/2 teaspoon each cumin, coriander, cinnamon. Smoked (or regular) paprika
- 1 pinch sea salt or juice (optional)
- Garlic herb sauce hummus
- 1/4 cup (or tahini)
- 1/2 medium lemon, juice (1/2 lemon yield ~ 1 tbsp juice)

- 3/4 - 1 teaspoon dill (or sub 2-3 teaspoons fresh per 3 / 4-1 teaspoon dried) dried
- 3 cloves garlic, minced (3 cloves yield ~ 1 1/2 teaspoons or 9 g)
- Water or sweet almond milk (thin to)
- Sea Salt (optional // I did not need any)
- Toppings, optional
- 1/4 cup cherry tomatoes (diced)
- 1/4 of Chopped parsley (minced)
- 2 tablespoons juice

Instructions

- The line to an external baking sheet with 400 degrees F (204 C) and preheat oven foil.
- Scrub the potatoes and cut them in half lengthwise. This can speed up cooking time. Otherwise, leave completely and bake longer (approximately twice the time (45 minutes - 1 hour).
- Put the steamed and dried chickpeas on a foil-lined baking sheet with vegetable oil and spices.)
- And touch the vegetable oil to the touch. Keep face on sweet potatoes to Gdansk the same baking sheet (or the number of other baking sheets on the size).
- Whole sweet potatoes and chickpeas roast are putting all the ingredients in a bowl and eat your shaking mix. Prepare her, just add enough water to the almond milk thin, so it is

wearable. Adjust the taste and adjust the season as per need. Add more garlic for more zing, salt for taste, juice for freshness, Dill for a more intense herb flavor. I found that I don't want anything.

- Note: If you don't, don't have the hummus, tahini (which you're DIY!) Sauce for. A would make an excellent base replacement - just provides the flavor tahini. Adjust the seasonings to accommodate the lack of flavor.
- Also, prepare the parsley-tomato topping by tossing with tomatoes and parsley to separate the juice and setting.
- Once the sweet potato thorns turn soft and so the chickpeas are golden brown - about 25 minutes - remove from the oven.
- To serve, flip the potato meat and press the insides slightly. Then top with chickpeas, sauce, and parsley-tomato garnish. Serve immediately.
- Additional side ideas may include hummus, pita chips, baba Ganesh or Persian eggplant dip. Enjoy it.

Shrimp Noodles

Ingredients

- 1 pound of shrimp with preferably Key West
- 1/3 cup plus 2 tablespoons vegetable oil
- 4 large cloves garlic peeled and pressed or minced
- salt and freshly ground black pepper

- 3 medium-sized zucchinis
- 1 12-oz ounce package DeLillo organic whole Wheat Linguine
- 3butter
- tablespoons1 lemon Z and juice (about 3 juice)
- flakestablespoons1 teaspoon red pepper
- grated 1/2 cup cheese
- Fresh chopped Italian parsley

Instructions

- Remove Rinse, tail Devin and shrimp. Add them to a medium-sized bowl. Drizzle with 1 teaspoon of vegetable oil and add 2 cloves of minced or pressed garlic. Season with kosher salt and freshly ground black pepper, toss with vegetable oil and garlic and set aside.
- Trim the ends of the zucchini and use a spiralizer to make the zucchini noodles. If you do not have a spiralizer, slice through thin coins or use a vegetable peel to make long ribbons.
- Boil an outside pot of water, then add a healthy amount of kosher salt to taste in the water. Cook the lignite consistent with the package directions, 2 minutes so that it is still hard. Use tongs to transfer the cooked language to a strainer and reserve the pasta water, bringing it to a slow, bubbling boil.
- In a large, high-sided pan or pan, add 1 tablespoon of vegetable oil to the pan over medium-high heat. Place the shrimp inside the pan and cook for two minutes, then turn the

shrimp in the opposite direction and cook for two more minutes or just opaque—transfer shrimp to a plate. Within the same pan, melt butter over medium-high heat and add the remaining 1/3 cup vegetable oil. Scrap the garlic pieces and add the remaining 2 minced or pressed garlic cloves, lemon rind, juice, red chili flakes, and 1/2 cup reserved pasta water. Cook for 1 minute, shaking once or twice.

- Dip the zucchini noodles in the pan. You cook the pasta with reserved pasta water and cook for 1 minute, stirring, just the rawness required for a long time. Use tongs to transfer the zucchini noodles to the pan with a mixture of vegetable oil and toss to coat. Add Parmesan Noodles and 1/4 cup Parmesan Cheese and toss to coat. To loosen the pasta, add 1/4 cup of reserved pasta water at a time, and you can make the sauce more if desired. Add shrimp to pasta and zucchini and season with more kosher salt and freshly ground black pepper to taste. Top with the remaining 1/4 cup Parmesan cheese and garnish with chopped Italian parsley and serve.

Pineapple Chalk Seth Jerk Shrimp

Ingredients

- 1 cup of water
- 1/2 Cain cup fruit juice (pineapple)
- 1 cup pineapple chunks, drained
- 1 tablespoon butter

- 1/4 teaspoon. Crushed red chili
- 1 tsp. Flavor
- 1/2 teaspoon. Garlic Powder
- 1/2 tsp. Onion powder
- 1/2 tsp. Salt
- 1 tbsp syrup, 100% pure
- 1 tbsp juice, freshly squeezed
- 1 cup basmati rice
- 2 to 4 tbsp ditophal, chopped
- for shrimp
- 2 cloves garlic,
- 2 tbsp butter
- 4 cups shrimp, small / baby size

Instructions

- Cookout rice in a medium-sized pot of water, fruit juice, pineapple chunks, butter, cayenne, flavoring, garlic powder, onion powder, salt, Add syrup, and juice. Bring the pot to a boil. Stir in the rice and keep boiling over medium-high heat.
- Reduce heat to a boil and canopy. Cook the rice for about 20 minutes until all the water is absorbed, and the rice becomes soft.
- Remove from heat and let the rice sit for 10 minutes. (Make shrimp in the meantime) When the rice is finished fluffing with a fork, stir in the cilantro.

- Shrimp
- During a large pan over medium-high heat. Stir in the garlic and cook for about 1-2 minutes or until fragrant. (Do not let the garlic burn).
- Reduce heat, stir in shrimp, and jerky masala. Cook the shrimp for about 2-3 minutes or until the shrimp turns pink.
- Heat with the desired amount of chopped green onions and toss the shrimp. Serve over rice.

Mediterranean Grilled Balsamic Chicken

Ingredients

- 2 Skinless Boneless Simple Truth Chicken Breast
- 1/4 Cup Vegetable Oil
- 1/4 Cup Golden Balsamic Vinegar
- 1/8 cup Private Selection Whole Grain Heal Garlic
- 1 1/2 Tbsp Linseed Vinegar
- 3 Cloves Garlic pressed Yakima minced
- 1/2 Nonbikers

- 1 fresh like a heap true meat herbs chopped tarragon rosemary or thyme
- 1 teaspoon kosher salt
- 1/2 teaspoon Aja ground pepper.

Instructions

- Trim any excess fat from chicken breasts and place in a bowl or gallon-sized freezer bags.
- In a small bowl, mix vegetable oil, balsamic vinegar, mustard, garlic, juice, herbs, and salt and pepper. Reserve half the pickle and add the opposite half to the bowl or bag with the chicken. Marinate overnight for at least half an hour, occasionally.
- When able to grill, bring the outside grill from one side to the other in high heat.
- The oil grinds the grill well and dripping the chicken breasts with more vegetable oil, then place the chicken breasts on the grill recently. Cook for 2-3 minutes or until grill marks appear, then flip the chicken and cook for 2-3 minutes. Grill, cover, and refrigerate to cool for 10 minutes. Transfer a couple of tablespoons of the reserved marinade to a separate bowl and use it to flip and flip the chicken. Continue cooking, baking and napping until the breasts have an indoor temperature of 165 degrees. Give the pigeon breast more grill marks and color to move the chicken over the recent edge of the grill, but make

sure to see them so that the balls in the marinade does not burn. The length of cooking time will be equal to the thickness of the breast, but you should calculate the entire cooking time for about half an hour.

- Transfer the chicken to a platter and canopy with a little aluminum foil and let it rest for five minutes. Serve with olive tapenade, Feta Cheese with any leftover pickle or vegetable oil served with minced herbs and drizzle.

Cheuk and Vegetable Coconut Curry

Ingredients

4 servings

- 1 Tbsp Extra-Virgin Vegetable Oil
- 1 Chive Onion, Finely Chopped
- 1 Red Bell Pepper, Thin
- 1 Tbsp Fresh Ginger, Minced
- 3 Garlic Cloves, Minced
- 1 Small Head Cauliflower, Diet bite-size Kefala.
- 2 tablespoons chili powder
- 1 teaspoon ground coriander
- 3 tablespoons red curry paste

- A 14-ounce coconut milk
- 1 lime, half
- 28 ounces leftover
- 1½ cups frozen
- Salt and freshly ground pepper
- Can be served by mixing catechu (optional)
- St cup Chopped fresh cilantro
- 4 scallions, finely chopped

Instructions

1. During a large pot, heat vegetable oil over medium heat. Add onions and bell peppers and sauté until tender, about 4 to five minutes. Add ginger and garlic for about 1 minute and fry until fragrant.

2. Add cauliflower and toss well to mix. Stir within the chili powder, coriander, and red curry paste, and cook until the entire mixture turns slightly black 1 minute.

3. Stir within the coconut milk and boil the mixture over medium-low heat. Cover the pot and still simmer until the cauliflower is tender 8 to 10 minutes.

4. Remove the lid and squeeze the juice into the curry, shaking the mixture well. Add chickpeas and peas, season with salt and pepper, and bring the mixture back to boil.

5. Serve with rice, if desired. Garnish each portion with 1 tbsp cilantro and 1 tbsp garnish.

Bowl with Shirak + Winter Greens

Ingredients

Faroe:

- 1 cup cooked Faroe
- 4 Shrike mushrooms, finely chopped
- 4 Brussels sprouts, halved and sliced
- 2 leaves curly kale, taut and
- 1 egg (locals can get these delivered by Urban Diggs)
- Olive oil for cooking

Chimichurri Sauce:

- 2 tablespoons wine vinegar
- 1/2 shallot, minced (about 1 heaping tablespoon)
- 2/3 cups vegetable oil
- 1/4 cup finely minced cilantro
- 1/4 cup finely minced parsley
- Salt to taste (Vancouver Check this smoked sea salt from the) Island Salt Company)

Instructions

- Pre-Cook, to follow the package instructions to the pharaoh. Ripe furrows are often kept within the fridge during a sealed container for up to five days. Is it available to build a replacement at night, or just eat it?
- In a small bowl, mix vinegar and therefore chopped boils, and let sit for about 20 minutes. Add remaining ingredients and mix well. The sauce is prepared to be used directly, but it is best if you will allow the mixture to take a seat for a few hours to allow the flavors to melt together.
- When able to prepare, place the faro cooked during a medium saucepan and add a pair of water. Cover the remaining ingredients on low heat while cooking. Heat a pan and add a tablespoon of vegetable oil. Cook until the sliced mushrooms are brown and take away from heat and keep aside. Next, add some more oil and cook the bananas

and Brussels for about two minutes, until they are bright green and soft. Remove and keep aside. Heat the pan with oil one more time and add the egg, cooking as desired.
- To serve, place the recent furrows in a serving bowl and add mushrooms, greens, and on top. Pour the sauce over the top generously, add salt and pepper at will and pour it inside. This recipe does one thing - just count what you are expecting at the table!

Zucchini Lasagna Rolls

Ingredients

- 3 large zucchinis, trimmed (about 4 pounds)
- 4 tablespoons extra-virgin vegetable oil,
- Teaspoon salt plus a pinch

- 2 cups tomatoes
- 1 teaspoon Italian seasoning
- Crushed 4 teaspoons minced garlic
- east small spoon crush. Red chili pepper
- 2 cups portion-skim ricotta cheese
- acted cup grated Parmesan cheese
- East spoon ground chili ground
- 1 cup chopped almonds

Instructions

Step 1: Position rack within the middle and upper third of the oven; Preheat 425 degrees F coat 2 rimmed baking sheets with cooking spray.

Step 2: Slice each zucchini into 1 / 4- to 1/8-inch thick strips. Discard any small or incorrectly sized pieces. You should have about 24 strips. Brush the strips with 3 tablespoons oil and sprinkle with 1/4 teaspoon salt. Place on a prepared baking sheet. Fry until softened, 20 to 25 minutes. Set aside to cool slightly.

Step 3: Lower the oven temperature to 350 degrees.

Step 4: In a large bowl, mix tomatoes, Italian seasoning, 2 tablespoons garlic, and crushed red chilies. Spread the mixture during a 9-by-13-inch baking dish. In a medium bowl, mix ricotta, parmesan, black pepper, and 1 teaspoon garlic.

Step 5: When the zucchini is cool enough to handle, spread one tablespoon of the ricotta mixture on each slice. Roll the slices and place them under the baking dish seam-side. Bake hot, 25 to half an hour.

Step 6: Meanwhile, keep almonds, remaining 1 teaspoon garlic, and so a small kitchen appliance, the remaining pinch of salt. The process from ground to rough food. Heat the remaining 1 tbsp oil in medium heat on medium heat. Almond mixing and baking, often stirring, light brown, and fragrant, for 1 to 2 minutes. Serve the lasagna rolls over the almond mixture.

Vegan Smoky Moussaka

Ingredients

Tomato Sauce:

- 1 (28-ounce) Tomatoes
- 1 tbsp ingredient

- 1 teaspoon syrup (optional)
- 2 onions, finely chopped
- 2 garlic cloves, finely chopped
- 12 ounces smoked tofu (firm)
- 1/8 tsp cinnamon
- 1/2 can be mixed. tsp salt
- 1/8 ground black pepper
- A pinch cayenne peppers

Eggplant:
- 3 medium-sized eggplants
- 1 tbsp vegetable oil

Bechamel:
- 2 and 1/2 cup almond milk
- 2 tbsp potato starch
- 2 tbsp nutritional yeast
- tsp salt
- 1/8 tsp ground. Nutmeg

Instructions

- Drain tomatoes in a bowl. Keep the juice.
- Cut plum tomatoes into small pieces and enhance the skeleton with their juices.

- Heat on medium heat until the sauce thickens for about 10 minutes.
- Stir in the ingredients, syrup, salt, pepper, and cinnamon and take away from heat.
- Wash and chop the eggplants into 1-inch thick slices, brush the slices with vegetable oil and sprinkle salt. In a large non-stick pan on medium heat, fry on each side until tender and golden brown. By counting on your skillet, you will fry about 5-6 slices at a time.
- Transfer slices of eggplant to paper towels.
- Heat a tablespoon of vegetable oil during a skillet over medium heat. Add onion and garlic, and cook until soft, about 7 minutes. Scramble the smoked tofu and raise the skillet, cook for about 5 minutes, shaking every 2 minutes. Add spaghetti sauce, mix until everything is combined, and takes away from heat.
- Preheat oven to 400 °.
- Arrange a layer of half eggplant slices (I used a 10-by-6-inch pan) during an increased baking dish. Cover with tomato/tofu sauce. Top with another layer of remaining eggplant slices.
- Pour the bechamel to the top and spread it evenly.
- Bake for 25-30 minutes until the top turns golden brown.
- Top with chopped parsley.

Salmon Souvlaki Bowls

Ingredients

Salmon Souvlaki:

- 1-pound fresh salmon 4 pieces
- 6 tbsp juice
- 3 tbsp vegetable oil
- 2 tbsp vinegar

- 1 tsp smoked paprika or regular paprika
- 1 tbsp fresh dill
- 1 tbsp fresh parsley
- 2 cloves minced garlic or Grated
- 1/2 teaspoon salt
- 1 teaspoon.

Bowls:

- 1 cup dry pearl couscous or taro
- 2 red chilies
- 1-inch zucchini digging 1/4 round
- 2 tablespoons vegetable oil
- 1 cup cherry tomatoes half-
- fermented chopped
- 2 cups 1/2 cup of nation feta crumble
- 4-8 ounces of cheese
- 1 lemon juice

Instructions

- In a medium-sized bowl, add juice, olive oil, balsamic vinegar, smoked paprika, dill Combine parsley, garlic, salt, and pepper. Add salmon and toss well, ensuring that the salmon is fully coated within the seasonings. Let sit for 10-15 minutes.

- In the meantime, cook the taro or pharos consistent with the package instructions.
- In a bowl, toss together red chili, zucchini, 2 tablespoons vegetable oil, salt + pepper. Toss well to coat the wedge.
- Heat your grill, grill pan, or skillet in medium-high heat.
- Place the salmon on a preheated grill and grill on all sides for about 3 minutes or until the salmon is cooked to your best doneness. Remove salmon from the grill. During an equivalent time, add bell peppers and zucchini, grill for 3-4 minutes, or four points per side. Remove everything from the grill.
- To assemble, divide couscous or faro between bowls or juices and drizzle with juice. Add grilled veggies, salmon, cherry tomatoes, cucumbers, olives, and feta cheese. Doll with tzatziki and garnish with fresh herbs.

Mediterranean Potato Hash with Asparagus, Chickpeas, and Illegal Eggs

Ingredients

- Private Reserve Extra virgin vegetable oil
- 1 small yellow onion, chopped
- 2 garlic cloves, chopped

- 2 russet potatoes, diced
- Salt and pepper
- 1 cup canned chickpeas, drained and dried and rinsed
- 1-liter baby asparagus, hard ends removed, 1 / 4-inch chopped into pieces
- 1 1/2 Ground
- Dispone stairsteps coriander powder
- 1 cup oregano
- 1 sweet paprika or smoked Paprika
- sugar
- 4 eggs (to be)
- 1 teaspoon white Vinegar
- 1 small red onion, finely chopped
- 2 Roma tomatoes, chopped
- 1/2 cup feta fall
- 1 cup chopped fresh parsley extracted Goji

Instructions

- Heat in a large cast-iron pan 1 1/2 tablespoons vegetable Talha Turn the heat to medium-high and add chopped onion, garlic, and potatoes. Season with salt and pepper. Cook for 5-7 minutes, stirring it until the potato turns soft (some potatoes can get a touch of a golden crust, which is nice!)

- Chop the asparagus, a touch more salt, and blacker Add chili, and hence spices. Stir to mix. Cook for 5-7 minutes. Reduce heat to keep potato hash hot; Stir regularly.
- Meanwhile, bring a medium pot of water to a medium bowl and add 1 teaspoon vinegar. Break eggs into a bowl. Shake the boiling water slowly and slowly slide the eggs inside. The white part of the egg should be whipped round and round. Cook properly for 3 minutes, then remove the eggs with boiling water and a short time with a kitchen towel. Season with salt and pepper.
- Remove potato hash from heat and add chopped red onion, tomato, feta, and parsley. Top with poached eggs. Enjoy it!

Mediterranean Nachos

Ingredients

4/6 servings

Vegetable Chips:

- 4 beets (mix of colors) and/or turnips
- 2 sweet potatoes

- Extra virgin vegetable oil
- Kosher
- Pickled chickpeas for salt
- 4 tablespoons extra virgin vegetable oil, split,
- 1 onion chopped
- 2 garlic cloves, minced
- 1 1/2 teaspoons ground cumin
- 1 1/2 teaspoon smoked Paprika
- 1 chickpea, dried and
- 1 cup of water
- 1/2 teaspoon salt Kosher can Himalaya

Tahini-Yogurt for The Sauce:
- 1 cup without milk yogurt
- 2 tablespoons tahini.
- 2 tablespoons fresh juice (1/4 lemon
- 1 clove,
- 1/4 teaspoon kosher salt.

Extra Ingredients:
- 1 large avocado,
- 1/3 cup feta cheese,
- 1/4 cup chopped kalamata or Moroccan olives, chestnuts,
- 2, green portions Toon

- 2 tablespoons chopped fresh herbs (mint, dill, cilantro, and/or parsley) chopped
- Eliminate Aleppo pepper and flaky sea salt.

Instructions

- 375% F. Preheat oven to 375 grams of root vegetables well, and with a mandolin Fried slices. Steamed vegetables to coat with vegetable oil and season with the place during a bowl, salt. (Red and work differently with yellow beets so that their color is bad.)
- A sheet Arrange the chopped vegetables on the pan with a rack placed above; bake for 25 to half an hour or until crisp and golden. Alternatively, you will place the chopped vegetables directly on a sheet pan and turn halfway through.
- Meanwhile, make spicy chickpeas: Heat half the vegetable oil in a saucepan on medium heat. Sauté onion until soft, about 7 to 9 minutes. Add garlic and spices and fry until fragrant, about one minute. Chole, water, and Add salt. Let the chickpeas cook until soft and most of the water has evaporated, about 20 minutes, stirring occasionally and ending the chickpeas with a spoon. Stir in the remaining vegetable oil.
- To make the yogurt-tahini sauce, combine all ingredients during a bowl or during a blender. (You want the sauce to

go a little slower so that you can drizzle easily, so if your yogurt is thick, add a tablespoon or two of water.)
- To serve, place the chips on a plate and serve with the chickpeas, yogurt sauce, and the remaining ingredients.

Avocado Tomato Gouda Soda Pizza

Ingredients

Soda Pizza Crust:

- 1 1/4 cups chickpea/garbanzo bean flour
- 1 1/4 cups cold water
- 1/4 tsp sea salt and each (as per taste)
- 2 tablespoons olives or avocado oil (1 large for heating pan spoon).
- 1 minced garlic (2 cloves)
- tsp 1 tsp onion powder or second herb seasoning of choice (optional). You will also use dried herbs here.

- 10 to the 12-inch pan to heat in the oven (cast iron works great. See note for size)

Soda Pizza Topping:
- 1 roam tomato chopped
- 1/2 avocado
- 2 oz gouda (thin). Goat milk Gowda also works. See notes for vegetarian options.
- 1/4 1/3 cup spaghetti sauce
- 2-3 tablespoons chopped green onion.
- sprouted greens (onion greens, cabbage, or broccoli) on top
- Sprinkle additional salt/pepper
- Red pepper flakes on top

Instructions

- Mix first your dough, 2tbsp Vegetable oil, water, and herbs/spices together. Until smooth. It is best to let it sit for 15-20 minutes at temperature.
- While the batter is sitting, preheat the oven on the broil. Keep your pan within the oven to heat for 10 minutes.
- While the pan is preheating, chop / chop your vegetables.
- Using oven mitts, remove the pan after 10 minutes.
- Add 1 tablespoon of oil in the pan and pour it around and pour into the pan. Gently pour in your chickpeas/soda solution. Tilt the pan so that the battery is full and even.

- Turn the oven to 425F to the right and place the pan back in the oven for 5-8 minutes. Just about the batter. If you are using a large pan, the pizza is going to be thin and may bake fast, so watch it for 5 minutes.
- Remove from the oven.
- Spread spaghetti sauce on top. Then add your chopped tomatoes and avocado. Place your gouda slices on top of tomatoes and avocado. The scallion can continue high; otherwise, you can wait for the feature at the last moment.
- Place back in the oven for 10-15 minutes until the cheese has melted, and so the soda bread is crispy and brown on the outside.
- Remove from the oven. You must be ready to slide the pizza crust on a stone or heat surface.
- Add a bunch of sprouts/microgreens on top than any additional toppings. More onion-like, salt/pepper to taste, and red pepper flakes.
- Drizzle vegetable oil on top. Slice and serve.

Conclusion

Thank you for making it through to the end of Mediterranean Diet Cookbook, let's hope it was informative and able to provide you with all of the tools you need to achieve your goals whatever they may be.

The objective of this guide is to help you discover all the benefits and alternatives of preparing Mediterranean Diet meals to easily learn how to prepare and plan healthy and balanced meals for every day of the week and to start saving time, money, calories and energy!
We also hope you will find the recipes we shared with you useful and enjoyable, on how to plan a balanced breakfast, lunch and dinner in a quick and easy way for the whole family.

Finally, if you found this book useful in any way, a review on Amazon is always appreciated!

Mediterranean Diet Air Fryer Cookbook

The Complete Air Fryer Cookbook for Beginners with Delicious, Easy & Healthy Mediterranean Diet Recipes to Lose Weight and Live a Healthy Lifestyle

Table of Contents

Chapter 1: An Introduction to The Mediterranean Diet..........................262

    Health Benefits of the Mediterranean Diet

    Myths and Facts about the Mediterranean Diet

    How to Make Changes

    Strengths of the Mediterranean Diet

    History of the Mediterranean Diet

    Studies and Research on the Mediterranean Diet

    The Mediterranean Lifestyle

Chapter 2: Advantages of the Mediterranean Diet and The Main Benefits of Using an Air Fryer..........................314

    The Main Benefits of The Mediterranean Diet

    Main Ingredients of the Mediterranean Diet and their Benefits

    Advantages and Disadvantages of the Mediterranean Diet

    Benefits of Combining an Air Fryer with a Low Carb Diet

Chapter 3: Example of A Balanced Meal Plan and Useful Tips That Will Help You Every Day..........................332

Example n.1

Example n.2

Chapter 4: Air Fried Mediterranean Breakfast Recipes..345

Air Fryer Sushi Roll

Thai Style Vegetarian Crab

Bite-Sized Blooming Onion

Hum Seth Portobello Mushrooms

Vegan Air Fryer Eggplant Parmesan

Crispy Baked Artichoke Fries

Vegetarian Corn Fritters

Vegan Bacon Wrapped Mini Breakfast Burritos

Meatless Monday Air Fryer Thai Veggie Bites

Classic Falafel

Chapter 5: Air Fried Mediterranean Lunch Recipes..375

Air Fryer Fish and Fries

Cheese Egg Rolls

Air Fryer Shrimp

Air Fryer Nashville Hot Chicken

Air Fryer Crispy Spring Rolls

Air Fryer Beef Swiss Bundles

Air Fryer Wasabi Crab

Air Fryer Hamburger Wellington

Air Fryer Loaded Pork Burritos

Air Fryer Green Tomato

Air Fryer Tortellini with Prosciutto

Air Fryer Herb and Cheese-Stuffed Burger

Air Fryer Turkey Croquettes

Air Fryer Bourbon Bacon Cinnamon Rolls

Air Fryer Coconut Shrimp and Sauce

Air Fryer Quentin-Bourbon Feather

Chapter 6: Air Fried Mediterranean Snack Recipes..420

Air Fryer Pizza

Air Fried Vegetables

Baked General Tso's Cauliflower

Crispy Baked Avocado Tacos

Baked Potatoes

Air Fryer Potato Chips

Buttermilk Fried Mushroom

Chapter 7: Air Fried Mediterranean Dinner Recipes..437

Air Fryer Blacken Fish Tacos

Air Fryer Coconut Chicken

Air Fryer Salmon Patties

Breaded Air Fryer Pork Chops

Air Fryer BBQ Ribs

Mexican-Style Air Fryer Stuffed Chicken Breast

Air Fryer Beef Wellington

Easy Air Fryer Pizza

Quinoa Air Fried Burger

Air Fried Unsaturated Veggies
Conclusion..467

Chapter 1: An Introduction to The Mediterranean Diet

When you consider Mediterranean food, your mind may indulge in pizza and pasta from Italy, or lobe chops from Greece, but these dishes do not fit into healthy diet plans advertised as "Mediterranean". A real Mediterranean diet is provided with the traditional fruits of the region, vegetables, beans, nuts, seafood, olive oil, and dairy - perhaps a glass or two of wine. Therefore, residents of Crete, Greece, and southern Italy ate Circa in 1960, when their chronic disease rates around the world were among the rock bottom and, despite only limited medical services, they had great anticipation.

And the real Mediterranean diet is about eating fresh, nutritious food. Daily physical activity and sharing food with others are important elements of the Mediterranean diet pyramid. Together, they will have a profound effect on your mood and psychological state and will foster a deep appreciation for the pleasure of eating healthy and delicious foods.

Of course, making changes to your diet is never easy, especially if you are trying to do away with the convenience of processed and takeout foods. But the Mediterranean diet is often cheaper and satisfying to eat and healthier. Making the switch from pepperoni and pasta to fish and avocado may take some effort, but you'll soon be on your way to a healthier and longer life.

Health Benefits of the Mediterranean Diet

A traditional Mediterranean diet consisting of many fresh fruits and vegetables, nuts, fish and olive oil - combined with physical activity - can reduce the risk of great mental and physical health problems by you: heart condition and stroke.

Following a Mediterranean diet limits your intake of refined bread, processed foods, and meat, and encourages drinking instead of hard liquor - all factors that will help prevent heart conditions and strokes.

Keep you tight If you are an older adult, the nutrients obtained with the Mediterranean diet can reduce your risk of developing muscle weakness and other symptoms of waste by about 70 percent.

Reducing Alzheimer's risk. Research suggests that Mediterranean diets can improve cholesterol, blood sugar levels and overall vessel health, which can progressively reduce the risk of Alzheimer's disease or dementia.

Reducing the risk of Parkinson's disease. High levels of antioxidants within the Mediterranean diet can prevent cells from undergoing a harmful process called oxidative stress, reducing the risk of Parkinson's disease by half.

Increasing longevity. By reducing your risk of developing heart conditions or cancer with a Mediterranean diet, you are reducing your risk of death by 20% at any age.

Prevention from type 2 diabetes The Mediterranean diet is rich in fiber that digests slowly, prevents a massive drop in blood sugar and can help you maintain a healthy weight.

Myths and Facts about the Mediterranean Diet

There are many benefits to post-, but there are still many misconceptions on how to cash in on a healthy, long life to capitalize on a lifestyle. The following are some myths and facts about the Mediterranean diet.

Myth 1: This method costs tons to eat.
Fact: If you are making a meal out of beans or lentils as your main source of protein, and are mostly studded with plants and whole grains, the Mediterranean diet is more expensive than serving packaged or processed foods.

Myth 2: If one glass of wine is sweet for your heart, then three glasses are 3 times healthy.

Fact: A moderate amount of wine (one drink each day for women; two for men) certainly has unique health benefits for your heart, but drinking in excess has other effects. Anything quite two glasses of wine can be bad for your heart.

Myth 3: Eating large bowls of pasta and bread is the Mediterranean way.

Fact: Usually, the Mediterranean does not eat a huge plate of pasta the way Americans do. Instead, pasta is typically a funeral with some 1/2-cup to 1-cup serving sizes. The remainder of their plate consists of lettuce, vegetables, fish or organic, grass-fed meat and a slice of bread.

Myth 4: The Mediterranean diet is only about food.

Fact: Food can be a big part of the diet, yes, but do not ignore the opposite ways to live a Mediterranean life. Once they sit for a meal, they do not sit in front of a TV or dine in a hurry; They sit with others to have a relaxed, leisurely meal, which can be as important for your health as it is on your plate. The Mediterranean also enjoys many physical activities.

How to Make Changes

If you're feeling crazy thinking about adjusting, you're eating habits to a Mediterranean diet, here are some tips that urge you to start:

Eat many vegetables, vegetable oil and icing Try an easy plate of chopped tomatoes dripped with crumbled cheese, or add your thin-crust pies with peppers and mushrooms instead of sausage and pepperoni Load Ga. Salads, soups and crudité platters are also great for loading on vegetables.

Always have breakfast Fruits, whole grains, and other fiber-rich foods are excellent thanks to the start of your day, keeping you pleasantly plentiful for hours.

Eat seafood twice every week. Fishes such as tuna, salmon, herring, sablefish (black cod), and sardines are rich in omega-3 fatty acids and shellfish such as muscles, oysters, and clams have similar benefits for brain and heart health.

Cook a vegetarian meal one night every week. If this is useful, you will hope for a trend of eating meat on the primary day of the week or just pick a place every day where you cook meals around beans, whole grains, and vegetables. Once you get the hang of it, try two nights every week.

Enjoy dairy products carefully. The USDA recommends limiting saturated fat to a very low 10% of your daily calories (about 200 calories for many people). It also allows you to enjoy dairy products like natural (unprocessed) cheese, Greek or plain yogurt.

For dessert, eat fresh fruit. Instead of frozen sweets, cakes, or other food, choose strawberries, fresh figs, grapes, or apples.

Use good fat. Extra-virgin vegetable oils, nuts, sunflower seeds, olives, and avocados are great sources of healthy fats for your daily diet.

What to try about mercury in fish?
Despite all the health benefits of seafood, almost all fish and shellfish have traces of pollutants, including toxic metal mercury. These guidelines can help you make the safest choice.

The concentration of mercury and other pollutants increases in larger fish, so it is best to avoid eating large fish such as sharks, swordfish, tilefish, and caveolae.
Most adults can safely eat 12 ounces (two 6-ounce servings) of other types of cooked seafood every week.
Pay attention to local seafood advice to find out if the fish you caught is safe to eat.

For pregnant, nursing mothers, and young women ages 12 and younger, choose fish and shellfish that are low in mercury, such as shrimp, canned light tuna, salmon, pollock, or catfish. Due to its high mercury content, do not eat 6 ounces (an average meal) of albacore tuna per week.

Make mealtime a social experience. The simple act of lecturing a lover or loved one on the dining table can play a big role in relieving stress and boosting mood. Eating with others can also prevent overeating; it is as healthy for your waist as it is for your attitude. Cut out the TV and computer, remove your smartphone, and hook up with someone during the meal.

Gather the family together and yet be awake with each other's daily lives. Regular family meals provide comfort to children and is an excellent thanks for keeping an eye on their eating habits as well.

Share food with others to expand your social network. If you live alone, cook a touch extra and invite a boyfriend, coworker, or neighbor to join you.

Cook with others. Invite a lover to share shopping and cooking responsibilities for Mediterranean food. Cooking with others is often thanks to deepening relationships and dividing prices, it can be cheaper for both of you.

Quick Start for Mediterranean Diet Mediterranean Diet

The easiest thanks to making changes are to start with small steps. You will do this:

Cook in vegetable oil instead of butter.

Enjoying salads as a starter or Antrim, eating more fruits and vegetables, snacking on fruits, and incorporating veggies into other dishes.

Choosing whole grains instead of refined bread, rice, and pasta.

Replacement of fish at least twice per week for meat.

Limit high-fat dairy by turning 2% or milk to skim or 1% milk.

Try this Mediterranean alternative:

chips, pretzels, crackers and ranch dip carrots, celery, broccoli and soda with stir-fried meat. White rice with quinoa mustard fried vegetables with light bread sandwiches or whole-wheat sandwich stuffing with ice cream made with halwa skim or 1% milk tortillas.

The Mediterranean Diet (Mediate), abundant in minimally processed plant-based foods, rich in vegetable-rich monounsaturated fats, but low in saturated fats, meats, and dairy products, is an ideal nutritional model for heart health. Methods of Mediterranean intervention trials, limitations within the quality of some meta-analyzes, and other issues may have raised recent controversies. It is unclear whether such limitations are important to attract Med Diet's post cardiovascular benefits. We aimed to review the current evidence on the role of Mediate in heart health. We systematically searched for observable perspective correlations and randomized controlled trials that were explicitly reported to assess the effect of Media on hard cardiovascular endpoints. We critically evaluated all earlier cohorts and randomized controlled trials included within the 5 most comprehensive meta-analysis published between 2014 and 2018 and additional prospective studies were not included in these meta-analyses, with a total of 45 reports of prospective studies (4 32 independent observational groups) including randomized controlled trials. We addressed prevalent controversies on methodology and other issues. Some departures from individual randomization during membership of the Landmark Spanish trial (PREDIMED [Prevention con Diet Mediterranean]) did not represent any clinically meaningful attenuation within the strength of their findings, and therefore PREDIMED's results were robust across a wide selection of sensitivities. Analyze. Work-because standards were met, and potential sources of controversy did not represent any reason to compromise most findings of available observational studies and randomized controlled trials. The available evidence is large, strong, and consistent. Better congruence with general mediate is related to better heart health outcomes, including clinically meaningful reductions in rates of coronary heart status, ischemic stroke, and total disorder.

Diet is traditionally considered a key determinant of heart health. One of the 7 heart health metrics proposed in 2010 by the American Heart Association (Simple 7 of Life) directly matches a healthy diet. But at the same time, the remaining 6 proposed health metrics (body mass index, vital signs, total cholesterol, and blood sugar) are closely determined by the other 4 dietary habits. Also, another health metric, physical activity, represents the exact opposite side of the energy balance equation and is indirectly associated with dietary energy intake. Therefore, a healthy diet is important to meet most of life's simple 7 goals and to ensure heart health.

In this context, the general quality of whole food patterns may be more important and more interpretable than analyzes focused on single nutrients or foods. The study of overall food patterns represents the current state of the art within the investigation of nutritional determinants of heart health. This approach is advantageous because it confounds different dietary factors and it captures the synergistic effects of different foods and nutrients. It is also going to provide a more powerful tool to assess the effect of dietary habits on heart health as the effect of a dietary element being too small to be detected in epidemiological studies or randomized controlled trials (RCTs) is. On the contrary, it seems logical that the cumulative effect of many different aspects of the diet is probably going to be quite large.

The Mediterranean Diet (Med Diet) represents an overall holistic dietary pattern in nutritional epidemiology that has been extensively studied, especially during the last 2 decades.

Med Diet is defined as a standard eating pattern found among populations living within the Mediterranean basin during the 50th and 60th centuries, but, unfortunately, not today. Meditates most characteristic at the time was a coffee consumption of meat and meat products, with very little consumption of meat (beef, pork, and lamb were reserved for special occasions only), processed meats, and very little butter. Or null consumption, ice cream, or other whole-fat dairy products (only fermented dairy products, cheese, and yogurt, consumed in moderate amounts). It presents a comparatively fat-rich profile due to the abundant consumption of vegetable oil, with high consumption of locally grown vegetables, fruits, nuts, legumes, and grains (mainly unrefined). 6 Protein Was an important source of A moderate consumption of fish and shellfish, which was variable counting at the proximity of the sea. Most sources of fat and alcohol among individuals within the traditional meditate are mainly extra virgin vegetable oil (EVOO) and alcohol, respectively. The abundant use of vegetable oil, along with salads, traditionally cooked vegetables and legumes, along with moderate consumption of wine during meals make this diet highly nutritious and tasty. Vines and EVOOs contain many bioactive polyphenols, oleocanthal, and resveratrol) with many anti-inflammatory properties. The post-antimicrobial properties of vegetable oil were reportedly attributed to the high content of monounsaturated fat (MUFA; oleic acid) and some new investigations also suggest that bioactive polyphenols are present only within EVOO, but vegetable oil Not within the sophisticated-common type of. May contribute to those cardioprotective functions. EVOO is the primary pressure product of black olive fruit and contains many antioxidants (polyphenols, tocopherols, and phytosterols). Low-quality oils (refined or common olive oil) are believed to be barren of most of those antioxidant, anti-inflammatory or pulmonary abilities as they are obtained by physical and chemical processes that contain fat but most of the bioactive Elements cause damage.

In the Spanish Landmark PREDIMED trial (Prevenient con data Mediterranean), which freed 7447 high-risk participants initially from the disorder (CVD), a 5-year intervention with Mediate significantly reduced the occurrence of an overall major CVD endpoint Which included non-fatal strokes. , Non-coronary heart condition (CHD), and every single fatal CVD event. However, the results of that test were recently withdrawn by S and simultaneously republished in the same journal. He included several new analyzes and addressed some of the smaller departures from individual randomization more broadly. Despite this, many questions remain as to whether Mediate can provide benefits for heart health in both Mediterranean and non-Mediterranean populations. It is also uncertain how variations within the components of the Mediate index used in various studies may affect this association. Additionally, other possible sources of bias must be adequately addressed.

In the first sections of this lesson, we will discuss some potential concerns about the beneficial cardiovascular effects of the Med Diet. Within the following sections, we will address the issues associated with these concerns. Currently, available evidence strongly supports Meditate as an ideal approach to heart health.

Possible limitations associated with the concept and operational definitions of
Med Diet an idea promoted primarily or partly for geo-romantic-indifferent reasons?
Many of the investigators who are currently strong supporters of Meditate have originated, lived, or have ancestry in Mediterranean countries. This may be a cause for concern as they would be biased when selecting pieces of evidence that best slot into the image of their prior perceptions of what a healthy diet should be. They are likely to include those aspects of their diet that they have loved since childhood and even learned from their grandparents or ancestors. It is easy to think that there may be a kind of mixture of scientific and fruitless reasons, many of them unconscious, during this group of investigators and these mixed motives may have contributed to their strong positions and opinions on cardiovascular benefits. Of meditate. This claim, as

discussed below, does not support the fact that many studies conducted in non-Mediterranean populations have found similar benefits of Mediterranean-type dietary patterns on CVD risk.

Is the Meditate idea supported by the vested business interests of vegetable oil and nuts companies?
The potential bias in biomedical investigations involving research funding by the pharmaceutical industry is largely studied and documented. It is well known that there is a large correlation between industry sponsorship and pro-industry findings. But similar biases associated with research funding by the food industry are only recently documented. Pro-industry bias in pharmaceutical research may have adverse health effects on many patients receiving medications, but in nutritional research, the pro-industry bias may be adverse health for all, with a substantial loss to public health. Will affect. Additionally, regulations for drug research are strict for nutrition research.

The scientific truth in the wilderness of academia — nothing more, nothing less — should be the first objective that everyone should pursue. This statement has often been repeated within the scientific environment surrounding investigators on nutrition and heart health. The first interest of multinational food companies is to expand their profits, and consequently, to make profitable food choices easier. Conversely, the first interest of public health is to make healthier choices easier. There is a transparent conflict of interest. Several published studies, particularly small trials with soft endpoints and reviews or comments on the advantages of Mediate for heart health, are funded by food industries or were written after their presentation at an industry-funded meeting. Although there is not a uniform range compared to sugar-sweetened beverages, this potential conflict of interest has been criticized, particularly about the concept of Mediate. BMJ's previous editor, Richard Smith, wrote, "A combination of vested interests, including the International Vegetable Oil Council and a PR company Old way, which promoted the diet, combined the diet with the natural charm of the Mediterranean." Popular ". However, these criticisms do not stand and support the fact that much of the evidence on Meditate has been publicly funded. We will discuss this issue during a later section.

Should refined grains be treated as mediate neighbors?
Currently available epidemiological evidence to consume less frequent refined grains and replace them by whole grain They support the advice. This replacement will reduce the risk of type 2 DM and CVD. However, within Mudit's most used operational definition, all grains are included as a positive item. There is no difference between refined and whole-grain grains. The idea that each one grain, including refined grains, provides cardiovascular protection, is the current scientific method. May be against the values. Modified the score developed by Trichoplax and included

only whole grain products within the Alternative Mediterranean Diet (Immediate) score.

Similarly, Panagiotis get much of the Mediate for very good consumption of whole grains. Followed by more. This modification seems more in line with current mainstream findings in nutritional science. The PREDIMED trial did not include grain consumption within the Meredith rearing regimen. This difference may make one suspect the reliability of some Mudit scores for capturing dietary patterns with the most significant potential for cardiovascular health.

Can alcohol still be a part of Mediate?

A moderate intake of alcohol is generally considered a positive item in most of the Mediate index. However, the results of a recent study have simultaneously acknowledged alcohol consumption as the major factor of the global disease burden. There is a view — based on some studies with inherent limitations — that alcohol, whenever moderately consumed, increases the risk of many diseases. A dose-response relationship probably exists between alcohol and various types of cancer. For this reason, some optimized Mudit scores excluded alcohol intake to assess the association between Mediate and carcinoma adherence. Thus, there is a question as to whether moderate alcohol consumption should not be used in the Meditates operational definition. Moderate consumption of alcohol with food is considered one of the components of Mediate, as discussed below, although alcohol intake is not encouraged for those who do not drink alcohol.

Do dairy products play any role within Med Diet?
The role of dairy products in cardiovascular health is controversial. However, for some dairy products, particularly fermented dairy products, metabolic benefits are reported during a nonspecific relationship, and a meta-analysis found significant reductions in the incidence of stroke-related to food consumption. Nevertheless, all dairy products are negatively weighted within the Mediate score proposed by Hristopoulos. However, those following amide and, therefore, Med Diet adherence excluded most dairy products with a null value. This is another source of discrepancy between the points often used in various studies that contribute to the idea that Mediate may be a broad term that varies in the literature.

Are Potatoes and Eggs a Neighborhood of Mediated Definition?
In all those definitions, potatoes were excluded from the vegetable group when calculating the mediate score. But potatoes with a smaller number of vegetables were included during the score, such as those employed by Tegan et al. And by Mozette et al. In the other 2 reports, they were positively weighted (supposedly beneficial) as they were included with grains.

Typically, egg consumption is not included in the definitions of meditation, but some studies included negative weight gain with meat or egg intake as a separate item.

Historical observational studies have previously noted that relating to mediate with cardiovascular mortality, 22S explicitly stated that potatoes and eggs should be kept separate from the rating system for the mediate, and thus received a zero consideration.

Should any diet rich in fruits and vegetables be the standard mediate?

Surprisingly, some meta-analyses categorized any Mediterranean dietary pattern as meeting a minimum of 2 criteria out of seven. The rationale for these criteria is quite controversial and this terminology is misleading because it means, for example, that any diet rich in fruits and vegetables can be called a Mediterranean-style diet.

What are the most sources of fat and fat subtypes within the Med Diet?

In the most common definition of Med Diet, the MUFA: saturated fat (SFA) ratio is one of 9 that wants to construct a score, but other scores have used it instead of unsaturated: SFA ratio, which includes polyunsaturated fat, which Much is attributed to the fact. Other sources of MUFA aside from vegetable oil are generally important in non-Mediterranean regions and so are the common finding of beneficial cardiovascular effects when SFA is replaced by fat. In other Mediterranean scores, instead of using the MUFA: SFA ratio, only vegetable oil consumption was selected for this item. Although vegetable oil will not correspond to the most important source of fat for heart health, the use of vegetable oil as the main culinary fat is an important feature of meditation. The PREDIMED trial gave EVOO a special significance as a source of bioactive polyphenols. These polyphenols are increasingly noted for cardiovascular health benefits due to their anti-inflammatory properties. Interestingly, the 14-item questionnaire used in PREDIMED was during an ll. Among each a> score that captured a very good intake of polyphenol antioxidant content compared to 21 Mediatizes.

Are polyphenols enough for a significant effect?
There are differences between the Mediterranean and non-Mediterranean countries regarding the types of flavonoids and food sources. But when a high polyphenol content of mediate is thought to be partially responsible for the cardiovascular benefits of this food pattern, a relevant question is usually raised: what is the minimum number of bioactive polyphenols, which yield meaningful clinical results but sufficiently large will increase the pulmonary effect. effect? The total polyphenol urinary excretion between substitutions of PREDIMED was measured and therefore the lower turtle upper limit of excretion was equal to 32 mg of acid per gram of creatinine. How is it possible that these

polyphenols, which are present only in minuscule amounts, may also make up for a powerful reduction in cardiovascular clinical events? This quantitative question that was important when postulating resveratrol because the main element responsible for the potential protective effect of wine has not been adequately investigated in terms of the entire number of polyphenols present within specific foods of Medicaid. However, polyphenols are a neighborhood of synergy between several beneficial bioactive compounds within the mediate.

Are sample-specific cutoff scores used to score certain median scores?
The general approach to achieving multiple adherence for Med Diet is to use the sample-specific mean of each food group's consumption and to specify a point for items that are at or above the sex-specific median of the sample for the item Huh. Consistent with the concept of common mediate. Conversely, a point is given to participants who are below the sex-specific mean of consumption for items related to general mediate. In other figures, sample medians used textiles instead of using bifurcation.

Indo-Mediterranean Trial Rare Reliability Indo-Mediterranean Trial Lancet
published in 2002,98 results, resulting in a dramatic decrease in the incidence of cardiovascular outcomes in 499 patients on a diet

rich in whole grains, fruits, vegetables, and walnuts. Compared to 501 controls allocated to the consumption of a field diet like almonds, a low-fat Phase I National Cholesterol Education Program diet. But later, in 2005, Lancet issued an expression of concern over the failure to locate the original research record. While this study has occasionally featured in both narrative and systematic reviews, it has been largely maligned and should be regarded as at least a critically flawed investigation.

Deviations from individual randomization protocols within the prescribed test The
Spanish PREDIMED trial included 7447 participants at high cardiovascular risk assigned to 1 of three diets: Medium supplemented with EVO, medicated supplemented with mixed nuts, or an impact diet (back Advice to scale) all subtypes of dietary fat). The trial was planned for six years, but it closed early after intervention for 4.8 years, as recommended by the Information and Security Monitoring Board because withholding regulations established a priority within the protocol. The incidence of CVD (MI, stroke, or cardiac death, a total of 288 events) within the Med Diet groups was 30% lower than in the control regimen.

Enrollment of household members (partner of a previous participant) without randomization; Random participants' household members were invited to participate and were allocated to a similar intervention group as their relatives. The second enrolled partners of the previous partner represented 5.7% of PREDIMED participants with a lower proportion in the control group (4.82%) than in the Minivet group + EVOO (6.72%) or Meditate group + nuts (5.54%). This was done to avoid assigning different diets to members of a different household. Handing over an equivalent diet to all participants in the household was the best way to realize diet changes within the home. This process was inadvertently left within the reporting of the protocol and, therefore, the original publication.

Baseline imbalance was slight and only included during a slightly higher percentage of girls within the control group (5.7% on top of things compared to the Mediate + Nuts group and 1% more on top of things than the Mediate + Ewe group) Within Med Diet + EVOO a 5.3% higher percentage of patients with higher levels of LDL-C (low-density lipoprotein cholesterol) within the control group. Interestingly, both are working against the hypothesis of litigation in either case and thus, this conclusion cannot provide any alternative non-explanatory description of the findings. Several criticisms were raised after the protocol revealed these departures.

The investigators of PREDIMED decided to withdraw their origin. And simultaneously republished a replacement addition within the same journal, where these issues were fully addressed.

The resurgence included results from several new sensitivity and ancillary analyzes that showed no change in terms of earlier results of PRIMED.

Strengths of the Mediterranean Diet

All previous considerations represent potential and pitfalls that threaten the validity of the Med Diet paradigm for heart health. There are also several strengths within the currently available evidence to support the validity of the proposal defending the Mediate model as it is an ideal approach to heart health.

Med Diet possesses a millennial tradition of use with no evidence of harm. Meditates current definitions are consistent with traditional food patterns during the 50s and 60s of the last century in the Mediterranean, where life expectancies after 45 years were among the best on the planet.

The pioneering epidemiological study supporting Meditate for heart health was not conducted within the Mediterranean region or by anyone living with Mediterranean ancestry. These first pieces of evidence came from studies in seven countries, and ecological, international, dietary investigation, and disorder in a total group of about 13 000 men in 7 countries (Greece, Italy, Japan, Finland, last Yugoslavia, the Netherlands, and) Were. Hence the United States). The study was started in 1958 by an

American investigator. It was he who developed and promoted the concept of cardioprotective mediate for the primary time. Therefore, it is unlikely that geographical-egocentric-romantic motivations associated with diet learned by some investigators in childhood from their grandparents may be based on this idea. Keynes was a physicist and epidemiologist at the University of Minnesota who discovered the mediates cardiovascular health benefits in the early 1950s, as a scientist about the rapidly increasing trend of coronary mortality within the Mediterranean. Countries visited. Keys did his first research on Mediate by studying men's dietary patterns and heart health in Italy, Spain, and Crete, with emphasis on dietary fat and fatty acid results on serum cholesterol levels and CVD risk. Their findings were particularly prominent regarding the importance of fat subtypes — and not total fat intake — and the relevance of the MUFA: SFA ratio. Meditate is relatively rich in fat (even up to 40% of calorie levels from fat), but with an optimal MUFA: SFA ratio appeared as an ideal model for heart health. These facts were by the long-standing experience of using this dietary pattern in relatively poor areas of the planet with high rates of smoking, and yet, with very low-CHD mortality.

Dietary pattern paradigms have several advantages. In contrast to the classical analytical approach of estimating exposure only for single nutrients or isolated foods, the study of overall dietary patterns has become the current prevailing framework in nutrition research. This approach has been fully adopted and supported by the 2015 Dietary Guidelines Advisory Committee. The pattern of food approach is beneficial for several reasons: because they can have synergistic or antagonistic effects after intake in combination with foods and nutrients; Composite eating patterns represent current practices found within current populations (people do not eat individual nutrients) and, therefore, they better capture particular risks of interest; They supply useful sociological information of great interest to public health in their own right; Use of dietary patterns because the relevant risk in nutrition reduces the ability to be confused by other dietary risks; And very importantly, the main goal on normal eating patterns seems to be superior to the reduces and all effects are attributed to one nutrient or food. It may seem unlikely that a single nutrient or food can have a sufficiently strong effect to alter rates of cardiac outcomes. Conversely, the summative effect of small changes in many foods and nutrients has a more biologically measurable and clinically meaningful effect. In fact, during the last 2 decades, several well-conducted prospective epidemiological studies have confirmed a strong relationship between a primary defined high-quality dietary pattern and a low risk of chronic disease, including cardiac clinical outcomes.

History of the Mediterranean Diet

The Mediterranean diet originates within the edible cultures of ancient civilizations, which evolved as the Mediterranean basin and vegetable oils (as the most sources of excess fat), plant foods (grains, fruits, vegetables, legumes, tree nuts) Is based on regular intake. , And seeds), balanced consumption of fish and seafood and dairy, and moderate-to-moderate alcohol (mostly red wine) intake by relatively limited use of meat and other meat products. A few decades ago, the Mediterranean diet attracted the eyes of medical professionals by offering expanded health benefits. The primary report explored cardiovascular protection, as several large-scale clinical studies, beginning with the Ansel Keys 'Seven Countries Study', showed a significant decrease in atherosclerotic clinical events in populations with Mediterranean dietary patterns. Forthcoming trials confirmed favorable effects on the risk of metabolic syndrome, obesity, type 2 DM, cancer, and neurodegenerative diseases. While its health benefits are universally recognized by medical professionals today, this state of the Mediterranean diet is challenged with great difficulties in applying this protective dietary pattern to other geographic and cultural regions and surviving it in the traditional Mediterranean Is kept, which is also affected by unhealthy eating. Habits brought by pronunciation around the world.

Traditional eating habits observed in geographic areas around the Mediterranean Sea, although differentiated by certain food choices and cooking practices specific to every country and culture, share a standard set of basic amenities. The exact dietary dimension of the Mediterranean lifestyle includes plant-based dishes using vegetable, vegetable, cereal, nuts, and legumes, most of which are cooked by adding substantial amounts of vegetable oil, with moderate use of fish, seafood, or dairy.

And limited intake of meat and alcohol (mostly wines). This unique dietary pattern came to be the result of a posh and multi-millennium interaction between natural food resources available within the Mediterranean environment and, therefore, the human element living in the Mediterranean basin throughout history. Become a precious medical device within the contemporary world within the last century

The combination of the term "Mediterranean Diet" and its success in the eyes of the medical public was made possible by the work of Ansel Keys, an American scientist. Primary to note the association between some traditional Mediterranean communities and the low incidence of the disorder in their specific dietary habits. Upcoming research confirmed the benefits by Mediterranean-derived dietary interventions not only within primary and secondary prevention of disorganization, but also within therapeutic approaches to obesity, type 2 diabetes, metabolic syndrome, cancer, or neurodegenerative diseases.

At a time when the recognition of the health benefits related to the Mediterranean diet has become universal, its irony is that its homeland areas are in danger of being extinguished. Globalization, the importation of Western habits, changes in lifestyles and therefore an environment specific to modern civilization have brought a significant toll on the general Mediterranean diet. At an equivalent time, when international guidelines include it in recommended healthy dietary patterns, the United Nations Educational, Scientific and Cultural Organization (UNESCO) considers the Mediterranean diet to be "the intangible cultural heritage of intensive protection". Given this conflicting stance between universal medical recognition and cultural extinction, the purpose of this paper is to review current information related to the establishment and development of the Mediterranean diet, the main medical evidence supporting its health benefits, and hence the challenges It has to be uprooted. To avoid erosion, to take care of survival and stability, and to serve public health with the simplest resources it can provide.

The term "Mediterranean diet" is employed today to explain the general dietary habits of neighboring countries of the Mediterranean, mostly Greece and southern Italy. Nevertheless, it should be understood to be quite strict about the preferences that these populations have displayed in their daily food selection because the first meaning of the word death in Greek is not just asking for food or food choices, but in a particular way. "living" better matches the fashionable concept of lifestyle.

The "Mediterranean point to the beginning of the diet is relatively hard, but the civilization morning basin, along with the outlandish population, has most likely evolved. Throughout history, the Mediterranean diet incorporated many of the habits brought by the conqueror, while keeping most of the previous local traditions alive and functional. The roots of the Mediterranean diet can also be found in ancient societies related to the Fertile Crescent - the Middle East geographic region that is the eastern end of the Mediterranean Sector Ice level position and therefore Mesopotamia, the Persian Gulf, including Canaan, and is consistent with northern Egypt.

The oldest of the Mediterranean foods among the basin countries and cultures. Hieroglyphic wine from Canaan records of ancient Egypt and olive exports are mentioned. The city-state of Athens depicted a fruit tree as its symbol, and so the ancient Greeks abandoned the offer of peace to humanity as an offering to peace. The Greek food influence was brought within the Middle East after Alexander conquered the region within the 4th century BC. As a plant-based diet, the Mediterranean diet received a sequential effect, as successive vegetation species were imported from other countries of the planet and acclimatized within the Mediterranean basin.

Food patterns on the Mediterranean coast were largely influenced by three main monotheistic beliefs that succeeded during the region: Judaism, Christianity, and Islam. These religions also adopted, kept alive, and held many of the essential components of the Mediterranean lifestyle as sacred.

The Mediterranean diet is not, in fact, a singular diet within the meaning of the word "diet". Each region within the Mediterranean basin developed its cuisine, preferences, and restrictions. The term "Mediterranean diet" can be understood as a specific "dietary pattern", in which specific characteristics are interrelated. Including certain foods contained within popular culture, ignoring the absence of other traditional foods or allowing the addition of foods related to other food cultures and patterns, should not be accepted as valid versions of the Mediterranean diet. An authentic Mediterranean dietary pattern should be viewed holistically, including all its characteristics, not just one of their neighborhoods. First, vegetable oil plays a central role within the cooking process, and thus, represents the most source of dietary fat. Cheese is employed in limited servings and usually within salads. Meat, milk, and eggs are consumed at a coffee frequency and in small quantities, and processed meat and sweets are practically non-existent. The Mediterranean diet, therefore, represents, in fact, the only traditional dietary pattern where consumption of saturated and trans fats is inherently minimal. Second, the consumption of vegetable oil is related to a better vegetable meal, cooked as a salad, and thermally prepared foods with an equally high beam intake, which means that the Mediterranean diet is a plant- Based dietary pattern. Other major components of the Mediterranean diet are whole grains, nuts, fresh fruits, and moderate fish intake. Grapes and their derivative products are also used, but one of the most characteristic features of the Mediterranean diet is that limited intake of alcohol, alcohol intake only with food, in small servings, with limited frequency throughout the week, and is done with consumption. Other alcoholic beverages such as alcohol or beer are not part of the normal lifestyle. However, some changes in food intake exist between different countries. For example, whole fat consumption varies substantially between Greece, where 40% or more of the entire daily calorie intake reaches a high figure, and Italy, where fat intake is up to 30% of daily calories, Is limited to moderate consumption. The consistent feature between different regions of the Mediterranean basin is the high proportion of monounsaturated to saturated fats, far exceeding the same proportion in Northern Europe or North America. Differences between countries also occur within the selection of other food sources. The Italian diet has superior pasta consumption, while the Spanish version of the Mediterranean diet features high fish and seafood. A literature review considering the differences between countries with a Mediterranean diet found that different from one case, three to nine vegetable servings, half to 2 fruit servings, from one to thirteen-grain servings, and eight vegetable oil combinations. Till every day. Although the amount of nutrients appears to vary, the number of different food servings, in most cases, substitutes for the different food groups complement each other, supplying the general unitary characteristics described above.

Studies and Research on the Mediterranean Diet

As a result of such geographic variations in food selection, diverse combinations of food groups are considered by current guidelines to create Mediterranean dietary patterns. The Diet Pyramid (a graphic representation of most principles within the diet, where foods allowed in large quantities are represented within the lower floors of the pyramid and restricted foods are pointed toward its top) to explain a Mediterranean diet today There are three main forms for Old ways Conservation and Exchange Trust Pyramid, Greek Nutritional Guidelines of the Common Mediterranean Diet, and Us Therefore Mediterranean Diet Foundation Pyramid. A number of these models maintained the characteristics of normal eating habits, while others were modified in time to increase suit supplies, food supplies, nutritional needs, and eating habits nowadays.

Ansel Keys is the person responsible for considering the health safety effects of the Mediterranean lifestyle and coining the term "Mediterranean diet". An expert in biology and animal physiology, Key focused on the physical body at the helm of Star Wars II, examining nutrition techniques designed to restore health after starvation. While specializing in starvation, the figures of morbidity and mortality in post-war Europe came under his eyes. He was surprised to note the main decline by acute coronary attacks in countries where famine led populations to limit their specific high-fat, high-calorie diet, and reversal trend when an equal country recovered after the war Happened and so the population changed feeding again. At an equivalent time, Keys became aware of a high incidence of heart attacks in middle-aged business people thriving within the US, when he suspected that diet may affect health and is particularly at risk for the disorder. During an era when the concept of risk factors had not yet arisen, the discovery study on heart conditions in Minnesota merchants was planned to become the primary prospective study on the disorder in the medical record.

While working at Oxford during a year's rest in 1951, he came to Southern Italy to hear of a very rare occurrence of a heart condition. Keys visited Naples and opened a transportable laboratory there. He soon agreed to corroborate previously heard stories about a low incidence of coronary ischemic disease and showed low cholesterol levels, which the locals had demonstrated. Key made similar evaluations in other European and African countries, gradually finding that diets rich in saturated fats were related to increased serum cholesterol levels and a higher risk for a coronary heart condition.

When Ansel Keyes first presented his dietary ideas on the condition of the heart at the World Health Organization's World Meeting in 1955, he was skeptical and challenged by world-renowned cardiologist Sir George Pickering to present additional evidence. Granted. Unable to do so for the immediate, he took it as an inspiration for style and implemented a search project that was to become the study of the so-called Seven Countries. They combined tobacco use, diet, physical activity, weight status, vital signs, pulse, lung capacity, blood cholesterol levels and electrocardiographic readings consisting of all men aged 40 to 59 at seven cohorts, a select few Live-in rural areas. Former Yugoslavia, Italy, Greece, Finland, Netherlands, US, and Japan. Yugoslavia was chosen to offer the possibility to review populations in the coastal and inland regions of the country with two different eating patterns. Italy was the country where Ansel Keys made his initial remarks on the low incidence of heart conditions within the setting of a distinct (albeit not yet named) Mediterranean lifestyle. Greece offered an opportunity to scale up the population with a high-fat diet, but with a low intake of saturated fat, as the main source of fat was vegetable oil containing monounsaturated fatty acids. Finland's population was well-off but exhibits a high incidence of heart disease and a high intake of saturated fat sources. The Netherlands was representative of a moderate dietary pattern, with mixed consumption of meat, butter, and vegetables. The US population sample was chosen as representative of the incidence of the high disorder and for its geographic stability over time. Japan offered the possibility to review the population with a diet with minimum dietary fat. A total of 12,763 subjects were screened. At 5 and 10 years, respectively, the study team returned to all or any of the populations that were initially investigated and picked up data about participants who had meanwhile experienced a coronary attack.

When medical data was presented for statistical analysis, the results showed significant differences between geographic regions. During this sequence, rock bottom rates were found in attack events in Crete, Japan, and Corfu. On the opposite end of the spectrum, very good rates were identified in Finland, with the US ranking second.

Direct comparisons between Crete and Finland showed the incidence of coronary attacks to be approximately 100 times higher within the latter (0.1% compared to 9.5%). Seventeen percent of Finnish had total cholesterol levels above 200 mg/dl, compared to only seventy percent Japanese. Dietary calories derived from total fat varied between 9% and 40% of the total daily intake, but these data were not always related to the occurrence of heart conditions, as Greece had the best total fat intake. Calories derived from saturated fat vary between 3% and

22%; The correspondence between the incidence of heart attack and saturated fat was convincing. Excess intake of saturated fat was documented to be related to an improved incidence of the disorder in Finland and our communities.

The study of seven countries had an observational design and limited power to demonstrate a cause-effect relationship. Keyes and his team became condensed on the association between total serum cholesterol levels and, therefore, the dietary factors affecting them, on the possibility that the Mediterranean dietary pattern had a beneficial effect on whole heart health. Although the intake countries study pointed to the connections that exist between eating habits and cardiovascular risk, the concept of a "Mediterranean diet" was kept within the background until the early 1990s.

The Lyon Diet Heart Study was a secondary prevention randomized controlled trial to assess the results of a contemporary, French-adapted version of the Mediterranean diet in patients already suffering from an acute myocardial infarction. Therefore, mimicking the characteristics of the Greek diet is naturally rich in omega-3 fatty acids, but poor in omega-6 linolenic acid, S decided to use rape oil with vegetable oil. As some surprise, the results of this research not only showed a 50% reduction of the latest acute coronary episodes but also discounted the number of latest cancer cases and all-cause mortality. The health benefits of the Mediterranean eating style can no longer be ignored, and so the concept of the "Mediterranean diet" entered the medical consciousness.

In the following years, the cardinal benefits of the Mediterranean diet became stronger. At the time of recruitment, 74,607 healthy participants from nine European countries, aged 60 or older, did not include a variant of the Mediterranean Diet Score, within the AQ Prospective Investigation (EPIC) Large Cooperation in Cancer and Nutrition (EPIC). To estimate adherence to the Mediterranean diet. The score was obtained by adding nine partials multiple 0s or 1s, representing the intake of nine specific dietary components, and thus varying between absolute 0 (lowest adherence) and 9 (highest adherence). After a 4-year follow-up, a 2-point increase within the values of this Mediterranean diet score was found to be related to a 33% decrease in cardiac death. Two other Spanish cohort studies, also because the Multinational Healthy Aging: A Longitudinal Study (HELL) project in Europe, confirm the association between better adherence to the Mediterranean diet and a lower number of cardiac events, also in primary prevention settings. A relaxation in heart incidence rate was also observed in several secondary prevention studies.

One of the more recent large trials to supply strong evidence in favor of the Mediterranean diet was the Spanish Prevention con diet Mediterranean (PREDIMED) study. Designed as a controlled randomized trial as the primary prevention, it enrolled 7447 subjects with no clinical signs of abstinence, including those advised to follow a diet group, and extra-virgin vegetable oil or Two active experimental groups were determined to follow a Mediterranean diet supplemented with mixed nuts. Although all three groups showed a small number of acute cardiovascular events, as all three diets had healthy cardioprotective eating patterns, the groups were randomized to a Mediterranean diet, yet with a potent 40, for the risk of cardiovascular complications. Within a 30% reduction was observed. % Reduction within stroke risk. Adherence to the Mediterranean diet was measured in PREDIMED with a hardcore, validated, 14-item screening tool (Mediterranean Diet Adherence Screener, or MADIT score) and found to be inversely related to the rate of heart events. Other analyzes on the PREDIMED study population showed that the Mediterranean diet appeared to reduce the expression of pro-atherogenic genes, cardiovascular risk surrogate markers such as waist-to-hip ratio, lipid fraction, lipoprotein particles, oxidative stress, and Characteristics of markers. Inflammation, but also the risk of developing metabolic syndrome and sort 2 diabetes.

Nevertheless, the initial clues from the PREDIMED study were challenged solely by the three intervention groups due to the low rates of cardiac events that could induce the statistically significant differences considering the incomplete randomization procedure, which Allows for biases within certain gases. Characteristics of basic groups. S chose to withdraw the primary publication and redistribute the information after the exclusion of web sites with randomization deviations; The result still showed significant reductions in the rate of heart events (within the group adhering to a supplement with 31% extra-virgin vegetable oil and within 28% of the group following a supplement with mixed nuts).

Attempts to adapt to the Mediterranean eating style and seek related cardiovascular benefits exist today beyond the boundaries of the Mediterranean. Indian patients with a pre-existing coronary heart condition or high heart risk were included in another randomized trial, a so-called "Indo-Mediterranean diet" that includes whole grains, fruits, vegetables, walnuts, almonds, mustard or soybean oil Is rich in To bring a higher content of omega-3 fatty acids, and compared the random effects group to a Phase I National Cholesterol Education Program (NCEP) diet. Patients who followed the "Indo-Mediterranean Diet" had a reduction in heart rate of approximately 60% and within risk for nonfatal myocardial infarction by about 50%. Adherence to the Mediterranean diet was related to a significantly lower rate of cardiovascular events during a large cohort study that measured 12.2 years of beneficial effects for 23,902 UK participants, as a statistical effect during the study, Significantly inferior treatment in PREDIMED is responsible for imperfection, a transferable ground in the limited transferability of dietary habits. Usage diet contained within the British population. Two studies within the

US have confirmed that significant decreases in the rate of heart events were also observed within the US population at high rates of adherence to the Mediterranean diet.

At the upper levels of the evidence pyramid, a gradual meta-analysis of previous cohort studies also acknowledged the association of the Mediterranean diet with lower rates of cardiac morbidity and mortality. A meta-analysis of randomized controlled trials comparing the effect of a Mediterranean diet versus a low-fat diet on cardiovascular risk factors showed significant benefits overweight, body mass index, vital signs, fasting glycemia, total cholesterol, and high-. Sensitive C-reactive proteins, with no significant differences in LDL (LDL) - cholesterol and HDL (HDL) -cholesterol levels. Another meta-analysis of the latent controlled trial examined the results of Mediterranean-like eating patterns within the primary prevention of the disorder and suggested gains on total and LDL-cholesterol levels.

Separate studies confirmed that adherence to the Mediterranean diet was related to the positive development of abdominal obesity, favorable weight change, and lower incidence of overweight and obesity. The protection provided by the Mediterranean diet against the occurrence of type 2 diabetes was confirmed by a scientific review and meta-analysis considering several dietary patterns. From the studies included during this meta-analysis, two prospective clinical trials, one in healthy volunteers and, therefore, in patients with a history of myocardial infarct, specifically estimated the benefits of the Mediterranean diet within the prevention of type 2 DM. Was designed to apply. Both tests found better adherence to the Mediterranean diet related to a lower risk of developing diabetes. A sub-analysis within the EPIC study described an inverse relationship between adherence to the Mediterranean diet and, therefore, the risk of developing diabetes. Already, the study of patients with type 2 diabetes was scanty, mostly cross-sectional and small-scale, which may explain why some of them prove an advantage of the Mediterranean diet over the criteria that evaluate glycemic control. Were ready, while others were neutral. The result is, however, no fatal effects were identified, and the benefit was confirmed in terms of decreased heart risk in type 2 diabetes patients. Nevertheless, several meta-analyses, including clinical trials in already diagnosed type 2 diabetes patients, also suggest a beneficial effect of the Mediterranean diet on glycemic control, the development of plasma glucose and glycated hemoglobin (HbA1c) levels.

Is evaluated by analyzes focus on potential benefits in other chronic diseases, following studies showing the protective effects of the Mediterranean diet against cardiovascular and metabolic diseases. A primary indication of a possible favorable effect of the Mediterranean diet on cancer morbidity and mortality was seen during a secondary analysis of the Lyon Diet Cardiac Study. The low rate of cancer death was then seen in several studies in the Swedish and American populations. With recent systematic reviews and meta-analyzes, improved adherence to the Mediterranean diet appears to have an inverse relationship with overall cancer mortality and, therefore, colorectal, breast, gastric, liver, head and neck, gallbladder and bile. There is a risk of duct cancer. Another focused review suggests a lower rate for the Mediterranean diet of all digestive cancers other than carcinoma. The EPIC study could be a large-scale prospective study in 10 European countries, including 521,468 adults who followed a period of 15 years for various cancers, cardiovascular, metabolic, neurodegeneration and nutritional outcomes; Research is ongoing in several working groups and current, or future publications are expected to shed light on pathways linking cancer and nutrition. For the immediate, some components of the Mediterranean diet were suggested to have a strong association with benefits within primary and secondary prevention of cancer.

Some data against non-alcoholic liver disease indicate a protective effect of the Mediterranean diet, with better adherence to the low severity of hepatic steatosis and lower levels of alanine — both cross-sectional and in some lower-numbers, Short term prospective study. Finally, the Mediterranean diet may not protect from the occurrence of neurodegenerative diseases. In European and US populations, and improved adherence to the Mediterranean diet was found to be related to lower risk for cognitive decline and the development of Alzheimer's disease. A prospective study on 131,368 participants within a health study of US health professionals and nurses showed that higher adherence scores to the Mediterranean diet were related to a 25% reduction in the risk of developing Parkinson's disease. Consistent with a 2014 systematic review and meta-analysis, an increased response to the Mediterranean diet was related to a 33% lower risk of mild cognitive impairment or Alzheimer's disease and a lower progression from mild cognitive impairment to a greater Alzheimer's disease.

The figures outlined earlier, coming from populations living in India, the UK and therefore us, are not the only attempts to adapt the Mediterranean diet to countries outside the Mediterranean basin. A 12-month longitudinal study on healthy Chilean male workers, in which the Mediterranean diet was applied within the workplace canteen, achieved improvements in waist circumference, HDL-cholesterol, and vital signs values, thus reducing the prevalence of metabolic syndrome by up to 35%. Another 2-year longitudinal study on obese Israeli workers randomly achieved significant weight, triglycerides, and total cholesterol reduction in a calorie-restricted Mediterranean diet; During another 4-year follow-up of the initial subjects, a low-fat diet was significantly more important in whole weight loss than that achieved by a diet or a low-carb diet, thus suggesting these metabolic benefits originate from a Could be better long term adherence.

During a set of studies on firefighting, a profession at high risk for cardio-metabolic disease, the greater weight of the Mediterranean diet, was related to significant improvements in LDL-cholesterol and HDL-cholesterol values, in total weight loss. With body fat cans, and the prevalence of metabolic syndrome and higher popularity scores and better adherence among Fire Service members. These figures can also be justified by the indulgent and attractive lifestyles that characterize the Mediterranean diet, which include neither total interrelationship in any food group, nor calorie count.

Attempts to understand the mechanisms involved within the positive effects of the Mediterranean diet on the risk of cardiometabolic, cognitive or neoplastic diseases cover an increasing number of publications in recent years. Perhaps the simplest thanks to explaining the advantages of the Mediterranean diet is to simultaneously explore it with the simplest examples of the concept of "food synergy", which may be a core element in modern nutrition. Different nutrients and foods present many interactions and mutually enhance their positive effects, in a measure that no different eating principles are often taken apart from the context of the whole dietary pattern or brought about by the Mediterranean diet Used as a separate explanation for the benefits taken. Altogether. In summary, the pathways are often organized as at least one or more of the effects of the Mediterranean diet on various diseases: lipid-lowering and modifying effects; Anti-inflammatory, anti-oxidative, and anti-aggregating effects; Modulation of hormones or growth factors such as cancer-prone mediators; Thanks to changes within the diet's amino alkanoic acid content compared to other eating styles, decreased stimulation of the hormonal or other- and intracellular circulating pathways involved within the development of metabolic diseases and cancer; Changes in the gut microbiota, driving a modified production of bacterial metabolites. A sub-analysis within the PREDIMED trial found that an improved polyphenol intake all correlated with lower mortality; A statistically significant difference was observed for stall ones and lignans, with no significant relationship between flavonoids or phenolic acids and overall mortality. Other data also arise from the PREDIMED trial which indicates advantages induced by consumption of upward amounts of vegetable oil within the diet; An increase of one-ten grams of extra-virgin vegetable oil per day was related to a tenth decrease in the rate of nonfatal heart events and a 7% decrease in the rate of cardiac deaths; The rate of cancer and all-cause deaths were not significantly affected during this report. Vegetable oil should be understood as a vegetable fat that mainly consists of monounsaturated fatty acids, such as monounsaturated fatty acids, but also polyunsaturated fatty acids such as linoleic acids. Since vegetable oil represents the most source of dietary fat (milk, butter, cream, cheese, or meat intake is significantly lower in traditional Mediterranean diets than in other eating patterns), it is used in cooking the entire amount of saturated fat. It allows as little as 8%, sometimes during the entire lifetime of a private. The high content in vegetable oil polyphenols and phytochemicals continues antioxidant actions and reduces the oxidation of unsaturated fatty acids in its composition. Also, the complete antioxidant capacity of the Mediterranean diet is met by the phytochemicals found in whole grains and antioxidant vitamins found in vegetables and fruits. In addition to vegetable oil, a healthy balance of fatty acids within the Mediterranean diet is met by the continued consumption of nuts, seeds, and whole grains, and polyunsaturated fatty acids brought on by moderate or high fish intake. The high content of vegetable fiber brought about by the rich consumption of whole grains, legumes, and fruits reduces insulin resistance, inhibits the absorption of cholesterol within the intestine and cholesterol synthesis within the liver, thus contributing to normal cardiovascular protection. Phytosterols made from nuts, whole grains, seeds, vegetables, and fruits also contribute to controlling intestinal absorption of cholesterol.

A systematic review of experimental studies examining the relationship between the Mediterranean diet and transcriptome activity in different tissues found evidence to support this association, although a comparatively small number of research papers were provided. In addition to the anti-inflammatory functions of monounsaturated fatty acids found in virgin vegetable oil, the peroxyl derivatives found in vegetable oil such as tyrosyl, and lignans also affect cell cycle expression, while oleanolic and malonic acids such as terpenes. The animal model has a modular effect on genes acting on the circadian punch.

The Mediterranean Lifestyle

Mediterranean Diet Nowadays: Between cultural erosion and worldwide recognition, like all opposite regions of the planet, Mediterranean countries were not prepared to reduce the current trend of globalization with all cultures, including those related to food. Worldwide, Bhudia is putting a clear seal on food choices, and the exchange of agricultural products, cuisines, and traditions has become a daily rule. As a Western food culture, technologies and advertising are driven by strong economic power; they tend to exert a marked influence on traditional eating habits and to substitute them in their traditional home as well. All this has been caused by the ever-increasing diseases related to excess weight and food and drink among the last generations of the Mediterranean-neighboring population. Lifestyle standardization, retailing development, low awareness and appreciation for traditional food cultures are left by modern generations, left in favor of the latest, socioeconomically driven changes, the integration of women into the market, thereby limiting culinary activities. Mediterranean food cultures appear to possess a function within erosion. Several surveys of dietary habits conducted in the Mediterranean were within the study of the first seven countries to participate in and characterized by low rates of cardiovascular events (Crete, Greece, Nicotra, Revelator and, Italy) of Mediterranean dietary traditions by increasing the decreasing effect. Reduced intakes of saturated fatty acids, animal foods, cakes, pies, cookies, and sweet drinks, and intakes of monounsaturated fatty acids. Of most concern is the low rate of adherence to the Mediterranean diet in many studies among children and adolescents in Cyprus and Greece.

Currently, environmental difficulties are challenging the sustainability of living Mediterranean life. Water scarcity in most Mediterranean-neighboring countries is driven by both decreased water availability and increased water needs, with agricultural demand currently accounting for 64% of entire water expenditure. Land wastage also has fatal consequences on food production. Reasons for land degradation include expansion of urbanization and associated infrastructure, industrial and solid waste pollution, wind and water degradation, salinization and alkalization, expansion of tourism-prone areas, sand encroachment, degradation of organic matter, all limited possibilities. Agricultural-soil expansion. There is also an echo of global climate change within the Mediterranean basin, as they induce not only water scarcity and land degradation but also the failure of crops, fisheries and livestock productions. Finally, species biodiversity is steadily declining within the Mediterranean (previously the wealthiest in the world) and with a negative impact on local agricultural production, an inclination towards monoculture and standardized farming practices is often seen.

Given the nutritional challenges facing today, the pyramid-form graphical representation of proper Mediterranean eating patterns had to vary to adapt to a world where obesity is driven by a sedentary and hypersaline lifestyle with an epidemic. For example, the Pyramids of the new Mediterranean Diet Foundation Expert Group introduced the concept of "staple food" to emphasize the importance of fertilizer consumption in each of those meals. Austerity and moderation are also advised on the sides of the pyramid. Other diet-related elements such as regular workouts, adequate rest, pleasure, and the importance of conviction and culinary activities seen as positive occupations, leading to high-esteem local habits, biodiversity, seasonal and therefore traditional, local use. Necessary. And environmentally friendly food products are also highlighted. Research is additionally aimed at evaluating the combined benefits achieved by combining Mediterranean eating patterns with systematic induction of weight loss. An external randomized clinical trial, PREDIMED-PLUS, performed by an equivalent team of Spanish investigators as PREDIMED and combined with a three-point weight-intervention using a similar type of Mediterranean-style dietary intervention, Randomization of 6874 participants ended in December 2016, with restrictions on energy intake, physical activity, recommendations, and behavior modification. And was predicted to close in March 2022; The design of the study, some foundational, and cross-sectional analysis in PREDIMED-PLUS have recently been published.

Struggling for stability and economic survival in their homes, the Mediterranean diet must also overcome obstacles in other regions of the planet, where its health benefits are recognized by the medical profession, but adoption by communities dominated by less healthy Westerners Limited thanks for the behavior. Countries in Northern Europe have started adopting the way the Mediterranean eats, thanks to the increasing availability of Mediterranean fruits and vegetables in local stores and well-run public health policies. The acquisition is restricted within the US, although modern nutritional guidelines have incorporated Mediterranean eating patterns into their appropriately healthy dietary patterns. Paradoxically enough, the Mediterranean diet is no longer considered a diet for the socially helpless classes, as it was immediately Ansel Keys made his first scientific observations, but a diet for people with a better socioeconomic status. However, the reality beneath this idea is not absolute. A better education level is more geared towards people learning about healthy foods, keeping in mind the dietary health advice coming from local and international cities and ultimately providing a better variability and diversity to their food choices Huh. However, when money spending is strictly talked about, Mediterranean diet prices are on the verge of a Westernized diet, as supplemental spending on fruits and vegetables is less than that spent on meat, sweets, sweets, and fast food. Occur. A prudent approach to applying Mediterranean eating habits to populations living elsewhere compared to Mediterranean coasts may be to look first for local dietary habits after taking an adapted nutrition survey, then these newly identified foods to spot, to match the pattern of the first Mediterranean diet. To adapt local habits for healthy Mediterranean people in some key points, without completely giving up on the main differences and exact character of local food cultures.

Chapter 2: Advantages of the Mediterranean Diet and The Main Benefits of Using an Air Fryer

It Is Good for Your Heart

"This is probably the most important known benefit," Moore says. "Mediterranean diet has been shown to reduce the risk of heart condition, stroke, and early death, all related to improved heart health." This is because this diet is high in heart-healthy omega-3s as an antioxidant from c-food, nuts, and vegetable oils, as well as all those fruits and vegetables.

It Enhances Brain Health

All those healthy fats are also good for your brain. A study with 1,864 participants found that those following a Mediterranean diet were less likely to experience Alzheimer's urge or experience other types of cognitive decline in adulthood. There is an immediate correlation between fish consumption and the low risk of Alzheimer's.

It Can Help with Depression and Anxiety

Due to psychiatrist and Well + Good Wellness counselor Drew Ramsey, MD is a vegetable and healthy fat-rich diet that makes it a part of their treatment for patients with depression, anxiety, or other psychiatric conditions: bananas, spinach, and eggs are great in your gut. Bacteria have been shown to spice up, and serially, your mood. One study found that when older adults followed the Mediterranean diet, they were less likely to experience depression.

This Can Help Stabilize Blood Sugar

Unlike other popular eating plans, the Mediterranean diet is big on whole grains and other healthy carbs - and comes with huge benefits. Says Beckman, "Complex whole-grain carbohydrates instead of refined grains, such as buckwheat, wheat berries, and quinoa, help maintain your blood sugar levels as well as help with all your energy. "

It Is Associated with Reducing the Risk of Cancer

When researchers examined a combined 27 studies - considering more than 2 million people - they found that the Med diet is that eating plans are associated with a lower risk of cancer ethics, particularly carcinoma, carcinoma, and gastric cancer.

It Promotes Healthy Weight Management

"Because of all the fiber, the Mediterranean diet is useful in managing fullness," Moore says. "You feel more satiated with foods high in fiber, which helps in healthy weight loss and metabolism." The key: replacing simple carbohydrates with fibrous fruits, vegetables, legumes, and beans.

It Has Special Benefits for Post-Menopausal Women

Mediterranean diet has also been linked to the positive effects of bone and muscle in post-menopausal women. This was little study, so more research is needed, but it is promising because previous studies have found that menopause can reduce the bone and muscle of women.

It Is Good for Your Stomach

One study has found that people who follow a Mediterranean diet have a better population of excellent bacteria in their microbiome than those who eat a standard Western diet. Researchers noted an increase in eating plant-based foods such as vegetables, fruits, and legumes, which put the great bacteria above 7 percent - not too shabby.

It Is Associated with Prolonged Stay

As if all the above benefits are not enough, it is also associated with living an extended life- mainly due to the above-mentioned better heart health. There is a reason why many of these "blue areas" are within the Mediterranean!

There is no single definition of a Mediterranean diet, but a group of scientists used the post-2015 basis of research.

Vegetables: Include 3 to 9 servings each day.

Fresh Fruit: Up to 2 servings each day.

Cereals: Most whole grains from 1 to 13 servings each day.

Oil: Up to eight servings of extra cold vegetable oil each day.

Fat - mostly unsaturated - makes up 37% of the entire calories. Unsaturated fat comes from plant sources, such as olives and avocados. The Mediterranean diet also provides 33 grams (g) of fiber each day.

The baseline diet for this study provides approximately 2,200 calories each day.

Main Ingredients of the Mediterranean Diet and their Benefits

Here are some sample ingredients that often include people within the Mediterranean diet.

Vegetables: tomatoes, peppers, onions, eggplants, zucchini, cucumber, leafy green vegetables, and others.

Fruits: Watermelon, apple, apricot, peach, orange, and lemon, and so on.

Beans: Beans, lentils, and chickpeas.

Nuts and seeds: almonds, walnuts, sunflower seeds, and cashews.

Unsaturated fats: vegetable oil, sunflower seed oil, olives, and avocado.

Dairy products: Cheese and yogurt are the most used dairy foods.

Grains: These are mostly whole grains and include wheat and rice along with bread along with many meals.

Fish: sardines and other oily fish, also in the form of oyster and other shellfish.

Poultry: Chicken or turkey.

Eggs: Chicken, quail and duck eggs.

Drinks: A person can drink alcohol carefully.

The Mediterranean diet does not include strong alcohol or carbonated and sweetened beverages. According to one definition, the diet limits meat and sweets, but 2 servings per week.

Healthy fats: Diets are low in saturated fat and high in monounsaturated fat. Health experts recommend limiting the intake of saturated fat to avoid high cholesterol, obesity, and disorder.

Fiber: A diet that consists of whole grains and legumes, as well as fresh fruits and vegetables, is high in fiber. Fiber promotes healthy digestion and reduces the risk of bowel cancer and disorder. It is also going to reduce the risk of type 2 diabetes.

Vitamins and minerals: Fruits and vegetables provide vitamins and minerals, which are essential for the healthy functioning of the body. Also, lean meat provides vitamin B-12, which is rare in a completely plant-based diet.

Antioxidant: Antioxidants include vitamins, minerals, and other molecules that will help remove free radicals from the body. Free radicals are toxic molecules that will form as a byproduct of metabolism and other processes. They will cause damage that will cause cancer and other diseases. Dietary antioxidants help protect the body by removing free radicals, and plant foods are good sources of antioxidants.

Low sugar: Fresh fruits provide natural sugar, but diets are low in added sugar. Added sugar is high in calories and increases the risk of obesity and its complications. The American Heart Association (AHA) recommends limiting the intake of added sugar to six teaspoons per day for women and 9 teaspoons per day for men. This is equal to 24 grams and 36 grams, respectively. Instead of sugar sweets, people will eat fruits on a Mediterranean diet.

The Mediterranean Diet Can Help Reduce Your Risk for Heart Conditions: Several studies show that the Mediterranean diet is sweet for your ticker, a meta-analysis published in November 2015 by the Journal for Review in Food Science and Nutrition.

A randomized clinical trial published in April 2013 within the New England Journal of Drugs in April 2013 provided perhaps the most convincing evidence. For nearly five years, Spain followed 7,000 women and men who had a high risk of type 2 diabetes or the disorder. Those who ate a calorie-unrestricted Mediterranean diet with extra-virgin vegetable oil or nuts had a 30 percent lower risk of cardiovascular events. The researchers did not recommend exercise to the participants.

The study reassessed information at a later point to deal with flaws widely criticized within the Randomization Protocol, and a similar report by June 2018 within the New England Journal of Drugs.

Eating the Mediterranean Diet can reduce women's risk of stroke.

We have already known that eating during the Mediterranean fashion may reduce the risk of eating disorders in some people. Well, the diet may also help reduce the risk of stroke in women, although researchers did not follow an equivalent lead for men, which is consistent with a cohort study published within the journal Stroke in September 2018.

Researchers examined a predominantly white group of 23,232 men and women aged between 40 and 77 living in the UK. The more closely a woman followed a Mediterranean diet, the lower her risk of stroke. However, the researchers did not see statistically significant clues for males. Most notably, in women who had a higher risk of stroke, following a diet reduced the likelihood of this health event by 20 percent.

Studies do not know the rationale for the difference, but they hypothesize that different types of stroke may play a role in men and women. Carson says an honest next step would be a clinical trial to understand the explanation behind the differences.

A Mediterranean diet can prevent cognitive decline and Alzheimer's disease. As a heart-healthy diet, Mediterranean eating patterns can also help reduce your memory and thinking skills decline with age. "The brain can be a very hungry organ. To provide all these nutrients and oxygen [that it needs], you've got an upscale blood supply. Therefore, people who are having a problem with their vascular health - their blood vessels - actually have an increased risk for developing problems with their brain so that it would be in the form of regular cognitive decline, "Keith Fargo, Ph.D., Director of Scientific Programs and Says. Outreach to the Alzheimer's Association.

What's more, funded by the National Institute on Aging. A small study published within the journal Neurology in E2018 examined brain scans for 70 people who initially had no signs of dementia and scored them in a way close to their food. The Mediterranean pattern Those who participated less often had beta-amyloid deposits (brain-related Alzheimer's disease-related protein plaques) at the top of the study and less energy within the brain. At least two years later, these individuals also showed a greater reduction in deposits and energy use - potentially indicating a greater risk for Alzheimer's - than they did. Who followed the Mediterranean diet more closely?

Advantages and Disadvantages of the Mediterranean Diet

Pros:

General

Nutrition Medium diet encourages the elimination of any food groups and the proliferation of nutrient-dense foods, making it easier to meet their nutritional needs.

Heart Health

scientists have conducted a strong amount of research on the Mediterranean diet and cardiovascular health, both also in the form of controlled trials in observational studies. A review study within the European Journal of Clinical Nutrition concluded that adherence to the Mediterranean diet is related to a lower risk of coronary heart condition, attack, and overall mortality.

Improved Blood Sugar Control

A systematic review found that the Mediterranean diet was poised to reduce hemoglobin A1C levels by 0.47 percent compared to the control diet. In the last three months, hemoglobin A1C shows blood sugar control in your body. Although it seems small, any deficiency can be helpful for people with diabetes who try to manage blood sugar levels.

Mental Health

A surprising benefit may be the relationship between the Mediterranean diet and improved psychological state, consistent with Kelly Toups, MLA, RD, LDN, Director of Nutrition for Oldways.

"A 2018 study in molecular psychiatry found that those most closely adhering to the Mediterranean diet were 33% less likely to develop incident depression than those not following the Mediterranean diet."

Also, consider the stress on social relations within the Mediterranean lifestyle. It is often paramount for the psychological state, especially in older adults. Loneliness can be reduced by maintaining friendship and regular social contact, which is considered positive for overall health.

Weight Management

It seems counter-intuitive that a diet that emphasizes calorie-dense vegetable oils and nuts can help with weight management. However, these saturated fats — recommended in conjunction with various fiber-rich vegetables and fruits — can help you feel fuller.

Reduces Inflammatory Markers

Inflammation can be a hot topic recently, as doctors and researchers establish a relationship between certain inflammatory markers and chronic disease. For example, two high-level inflammatory markers (interleukin 6 and C reactive protein) are thought to be related to an increased risk of diabetes. Research suggests that the Mediterranean diet is related to lower levels of those inflammatory markers.

Cancer Prevention

Most cases of cancer are not caused by a singular factor, but by a mixture of several genetic and environmental factors. Diet may play a role during this complex disease, and some dietary patterns — including the Mediterranean diet — are related to lower risk of cancer.

For example, a meta-analysis found that those who followed the Mediterranean diet most closely included colorectal cancer, carcinoma, gastric cancer, liver cancer of the liver, head and neck cancer, and the development of prostatic adenocarcinoma. There was a risk.

Cons:

There are only a few cons to the Mediterranean diet, as it is quite balanced and well researched. However, there can also be a couple of challenges to beat.

Price

Although branded foods or special supplements are not, some consumers regularly worry about the value of including fish. Seafood tends to be costlier than other proteins. However, there are many ways to buy on a budget - even for seafood.

Additional Guidance may also Be Necessary for Diabetics

although studies suggest that a Mediterranean diet may reduce diabetes risk and better control blood sugar - some people with diabetes may have additional guidance on this diet. Because there is stress on grains, fruits, and vegetables (including starchy vegetables), food can also be high in carbohydrates. People with diabetes need to consume an equal, controlled amount of carbohydrate throughout the day to avoid blood-sugar glucose.

High-fiber Diets May Help Control Diabetes

The Mediterranean diet is high in fiber-rich foods, which are said to aid in regulating blood sugar by absorbing blood sugar.

This, in turn, can help prevent and manage type 2 diabetes, the common type of diabetes.

The Mediterranean diet encourages consumption of nutrient-dense foods and the top ingredient

Dynan explained that the Mediterranean diet promotes consumption of whole plant-based foods such as vegetables, fresh fruits, whole grains, legumes, and nuts. They stated that these foods guarantee a high intake of important minerals, vitamins, and phytonutrients, suggesting a supply of beneficial effects on metabolic and inflammatory risk parameters.

Dynan also told insider that the Mediterranean diet concentrates on whole foods and eliminates low-quality, highly processed foods that are often full of additives, sugar, and unhealthy fats.

This diet plan allows you to interrupt and luxuriate food

"Diet on said that the Mediterranean diet is not just about food." The Mediterranean diet, she explained, advocates for us to interrupt, enjoy food and engage with our food and, therefore, the people with whom we taste it.

However, the diet has no calorie guidelines

"because there's no limit, it's often difficult to not have a selected plan or calorie guidelines". Also, since the focus is on healthy fats and whole grains, he explained that overwriting is possible. Additionally, she said that this diet promotes eating whole foods, like full-fat dairy products, which, if eaten in large amounts, can be very dense.

Benefits of Combining an Air Fryer with a Low Carb Diet

Here are some ways an air fryer complements a low carb diet:

- You can enjoy fried foods without carbs.
- It makes cooking reception fast and easy.
- Versatile cooking keeps things interesting.

Enjoy Fried Foods on a low carb diet. Fried foods are very unhealthy and a natural part of any diet. But air fryers turn to that. Their revolutionary cooking method allows you to realize crispy, fried foods without added oil. It makes it possible to enjoy fried foods by sticking with a diet.

Opt for a low carb option when frying foods for the keto diet. Walnut flour is an excellent alternative to low carb breakers. For a touch, extra texture, try finely chopped nuts instead of employing nut flour. Spray or toss foods with a saturated or monounsaturated cooking fat such as avocado oil, copra oil, or macadamia oil.

Chapter 3: Example of A Balanced Meal Plan and Useful Tips That Will Help You Every Day

Below you can find some weekly sample menus of the Mediterranean diet.

Feel free to regulate portions and food choices that support your own needs and preferences.

Example n.1

Monday

Breakfast:

Greek yogurt with strawberries and oats.

Lunch:

Whole grain sandwiches with vegetables.

Dinner:

A tuna fish salad dressed in vegetable oil. A little fruit for dessert.

Tuesday

Breakfast:

Oatmeal with Raisins.

Lunch:

Leftover tuna fish salad before night.

Dinner:

Salad with tomatoes, olives, and feta cheese.

Wednesday

Breakfast:

Omelet with vegetable, tomato, and onion. Some fruit.

Lunch:

Whole grain sandwiches with cheese and fresh vegetables.

Dinner:

Mediterranean Lasagna.

Thursday

Breakfast:

Yogurt with sliced fruits and nuts.

Lunch:

Leftover laze from the night before.

Dinner:

Served with brewed salmon, rice and vegetables.

Friday

Breakfast:

Eggs and vegetables, fried in vegetable oil.

Lunch:

Greek yogurt with strawberries, oats, and nuts.

Dinner: Grilled lamb, salad and potatoes.

Saturday

Breakfast:

Oatmeal with raisins, nuts and an apple.

Lunch:

Whole grain sandwiches with vegetables.

Dinner:

Mediterranean pizza made with whole wheat, topped with cheese, vegetables, and olives.

Sunday

Breakfast:

Omelet with vegetables and olives.

Lunch:

Leftover pizza before night.

Dinner:

Grilled chicken, with vegetables and a potato. Fruit for dessert.

Example n.2

Day 1

Breakfast:

A pan-fried egg

Whole-wheat toast for grilled tomatoes

For extra calories add another egg or some chopped avocado

Lunch:

Mixed with cherry tomatoes and olives on top Salad greens 2 cups and a dressing of wholegrain oil and vinegar.

Whole-grain pita bread

2 ounces of hummus (oz)

Dinner:

Spaghetti sauce, grilled vegetables and low-fat whole-grain pizzas topping for added cheese

For extra calories add some chopped chicken, ham, tuna or pine nuts to the pizza

Day 2

Breakfast:

1 cup Greek yogurt

Half a cup of fruit, such as blueberries, raspberries, or sliced nectar

For extra calories add 1-2 ounces of almonds or walnuts

Lunch:

Grilled vegetables, eggplant, zucchini, capsicum, onion, and the like whole grain

For extra calories add stuffing to increase calories: you can use hummus or avocado smeared on the bread

Dinner:

A portion of baked cod with garlic and black pepper

Add to taste a roasted potato along with vegetable oil and chives.

Day 3

Breakfast:

1 cup of whole-grain oats with date

Fruits with less sugar, such as raspberries

1 oz of chopped almonds (optional)

Lunch:

Boiled white beans with spices, such as laurel, garlic, and cumin

1 cup arugula One With a vegetable oil dressing and toppings of tomato, cucumber, and feta cheese

Dinner:

Half Cup Grain Pasta with Spaghetti Sauce, Olive Oil, and Grilled Vegetables

Parmesan Cheesecake 1 tbsp

Day 4

Breakfast:

Capsicum, onion, tomato and two eggs clash with 1 oz of top queso fresco or a quarter of an avocado

Lunch:

Anchovies with a sprinkling of juice on whole-grain toast in roasted vegetable oil

A warm salad consisting of 2 cups of boiled bananas and tomatoes

Dinner:

2 teaspoons of boiled spinach juice and herbs, vegetable oil with boiled artisan with garlic powder and salt

For extra calories add another artichoke to get a hearty meal

Day 5

Breakfast:

1 cup of Greek yogurt with Cinnamon and Shishir honey, sliced apples and chopped almonds

Lunch:

Bell pepper, dried tomatoes with 1 cup quinoa olive sun

Garbanzo beans wishful of Areaway leaf parsley, roast the feta cheese

Crumbles Sathish avocado (optional)

Dinner:

2 cups steamed black tomato, cucumber, olives, juice, parmesan cheese and a piece of grilled sardines with lemon slices

Day 6

Breakfast:

Two slices of whole-grain toast with soft cheese. queso fresco, or chevre

Chopped blueberries or figs

Lunch:

Greens mixed with tomatoes, 2 cups of cucumber vegetable oil and a small portion of roasted chicken with a sprinkling of juices

Dinner:

Oven-Roasted Vegetables, such as:

- Artichoke
- Carrot
- Zucchini
- Eggplant
- Sweet Potato
- Tomatoes

Day 7

Breakfast:

Cinnamon grains, seeds and whole grains with palm trees, and low-sugar fruits, such as raspberry or blackberry.

Lunch:

Stuffed Zucchini, Yellow Squash, Onion, and Tomato and Herb Sauce

Dinner:

2 cups of greens, such as arugula or spinach, tomatoes, olives, and a small portion of white fish with the leftover vegetable stew of lunch with vegetable oil.

Chapter 4: Air Fried Mediterranean Breakfast Recipes

Air Fryer Sushi Roll

Ingredients

For Salad Cal:
- 1 1/2 cups chopped - remove ribs
- 1/2 teaspoon rice vinegar
- 3/4 teaspoon toasted vegetable oil
- 1/8 teaspoon garlic powder

- 1/4 teaspoon ground ginger
- 3/4 teaspoon Soy
- 1 tablespoon sesame seeds - toasted or not - your phone!

for Kale Salad Sushi Roll:

- 1 Batch Autoclave Sushi Rice Chilled to
- Sushi Nori
- Hass Avocado 1/2- Sliced used
- Temperature Mayo Banas Vezina
- Make for the coating to 1/2 cup panko breadcrumbs

Instructions

- Kale salad combines, in a large bowl, vinegar, vegetable oil, garlic powder, ginger, and soy. With clean hands, massage the bud until it turns bright green. Stir within sesame seeds and set aside.
- Make black salad sushi rolls Spread Of naughty
- A sheet on a dry surface. With slightly moist fingers, grab a pair of rice and spread it on the nori. It is thought that the thin layer of rice must be covered with almost the entire sheet. With an edge, you want the naked seaweed to move about 1/2 "away. Consider this because the flap that will take off your roll.
- Unlike that naked part on top of the seaweed, about 2-3. Lie. Top with tablespoons of kale salad and a few slices of

avocado. Start at the top with the filling, roll your sushi, press gently to insist on a pleasant, tight roll. Once you at the top. Use that naked little one. Seaweed to seal off the rolls. If necessary, wet your fingers, and let it Wet a little seaweed to

- Repeat 2-3 steps to roll more than 3 sushi rolls.
- Make casserole taco mayo in raita
- Mix the shallow bowl. Fast the mayo with the, until you reach that warm level. Add more 1/2 teaspoon at a time until you find the spicy mayo.
- Fry slices
- Grab your first sushi roll, and coat it as evenly as possible within Sri Krishna, then within Panko. Put the roll in your air fryer basket. Repeat with the remainder of your sushi roll.
- Air fry at 390F for 10 minutes, shaking gently after 5 minutes.
- When the roll is cooled enough to handle, grab an upright knife and gently cut the roll into 6-8 pieces. When you are slicing, consider the saw gently, and do not press it hard with your knife. Which will only send bananas and avocados flying through the ends of your roll?
- Serve soy with a needle

Thai Style Vegetarian Crab

Ingredients

- 400 g / 4 cup Dieted or about 4 medium potatoes
- 1 bunch green onion
- 1 lime, zest, and juice
- 1½ inch fresh ginger
- 1 tbsp tamari, or soy

- 4 tbsp Thai red curry paste
- 1 x 398 g palm hearts, drained, long tubular shaped ones work best. (Dry weight at approx. 200g)
- 100g / can cup canned artichoke hearts, dried
- black pepper, to salt to taste
- 2 tablespoons oil for frying the pan, peel the optional

Instructions

- Cube the potatoes and then pan them. Add to Cover with water and boil until the boils are tender and mashable but not too soft, then drain, mash and keep aside.
- While the potatoes are boiling, add green onion, juice, lime zest, ginger, tamarind, and curry paste to a kitchen appliance. Break the nori sheets into manageable pieces and insert them within the kitchen appliance with contrasting material. Process until there is a paste. Nori remains a touch chunkier than everything else, which is fine.
- Dry the palm hearts well, and either grates them or mix them with a fork, then cut the artichokes and coarsely. Be sure to empty them thoroughly and provide a touch squeeze to the artichokes to insist any residual liquid in them.
- Once the potato has cooled down enough to handle, add the pasta and shake well so that it is evenly distributed

then add the sliced heart of the palm and so the sliced artichoke and shake gently.
- Form in the patties and place them on a tray with some baking parchment as they go. You will either pan-fry them, bake the oven or cook them on a grate to cook. They are the best pan-fried as they develop a brilliant golden crust.
- To pan-fry,
- heat a few tablespoons of oil during a pan over medium-high heat. Once hot, add crab cake carefully. Leave them well alone for about 4 minutes to allow a thick, golden layer to develop, then flip over and equalize in the opposite direction. Remove from the pan and put them on some kitchen paper to absorb excess oil. Your pan may not be large enough to cook all of them directly, so keep the oven on low and cook the cooked ones to stay warm.
- Let's
- heat your puzzle for medium-high heat. When hot, carefully place the crab cakes on the grill and cook from all sides for 4-5 minutes.
- To bake the oven, place it
- lightly on a baking parchment tray and bake at 400 ° F for about 25 minutes. Turn halfway.

Bite-Sized Blooming Onion

Ingredients

- 2 pounds cipollini onion, peeled and sectioned
- 2 large eggs
- 1 cup buttermilk
- 2 cups all-purpose flour
- 1 tbsp paprika
- 1 tbsp kosher salt
- 1 tbsp pepper
- 1 tsp garlic powder
- 1 tsp red chili
- vegetable oil, for frying

- 1/4 cup mayo
- 1/4 cup sour cream
- 1 tablespoon ketchup
- 1/2 teaspoon peripheral chic spoonful of salt

Instructions

- The first part often ensures that You can buy the appropriate onions! You cannot use frozen onions or pearl onions. They are a touch too small. You will like these cipollini onions. You will usually find them by the pound in most supermarkets near onions!
- Generally, once you make an outer-blossom onion, you will want to leave the base for the whole thing to stick together. I was born here because I wanted the onions to stick together, but it should be ready to eat in one bite as well and there is no need to worry about the base. I decided to isolate Aadhaar and see how it goes.
- Looks like you'll do it! Trim just enough to spruce up the dirty root but keep the maximum volume intact. Instead, keep the tip end intact! Then peel the onion with just a sharp paper; otherwise, you lick your fingers.
- Next, slice through onions to form squares (such as within the full-size version). If you don't get what you want for the base section, the tip section will hold the onion together. It won't work with a full-sized onion but works fine with

smaller ones. Just take care not to cut it all the way. A spiked knife helps!
- The Real Thing: This is often a very annoying presentation. I did a few tunes, though and worked through two pounds of onions in about a quarter of an hour. As soon as you hang it, they are going fast.

Hum Seth Portobello Mushrooms

Ingredients

- Vinegar
- Salt and pepper
- 4 tablespoons free spaghetti sauce (such as 365 organics)
- 1 clove garlic,
- Oil 3 minutes zucchini, sliced, chopped, or Julienned (about 1/2 medium))
- 2 tablespoons sweet,
- 4 flour kalamata olives,
- 1 teaspoon of dried basil
- Pepper minced 1/2 cup (see note for kalamata version),

- Minced fresh basil leaves or other herbs or happened, then minced

Instructions

- Wash the portobellos thoroughly. Stop the stems and remove the gills with a spoon. Dry and brush the pats or spray each side with balsamic vinegar. Sprinkle inside with salt and pepper.

- Spread 1 tbsp of spaghetti sauce inside each mushroom and sprinkle with garlic.

Air Fryer Instructions:

- Preheat the 330F to the air fryer. Use a rack to move a slot or two layers to as many mushrooms as possible. (You may have to try doing this in batches counting on dimensions or your air fryer and portobellos.) Air fry for 3 minutes.
- Remove the mushrooms and all with equal portions of zucchini, peppers, and olives and sprinkle with dried basil and salt and pepper. Return to the air fryer for 3 minutes. Check mushrooms and employ a rack if. Return to the air fryer for an additional 3 minutes or until the mushrooms are tender. Place on a plate, drizzle with hummus and

sprinkle with basil or other herbs. If you wish, you will put the Port Propeller in the air again to heat the Humor.
- Preheat oven instructions 400F.
- Place the fried portobellos during a baking dish and bake for five minutes. Remove from the oven and sprinkle all with equal portions of zucchini, peppers, and olives, and with dried basil and salt and pepper. Return to the oven and cook until the mushrooms are tender. Place on a plate, drizzle with hummus and sprinkle with basil or other herbs. If you wish, you will warm the humus by briefly putting the portobellos under the broiler.

Notes:

Kalamata is straightforward to make hummus and makes a delicious topping for these individual pizzas. Simply make a batch of hummus within the blender, remove half of it to use normally, and add 8–10 kalamata olives to the remaining humus within the blender. Blend well.

Vegan Air Fryer Eggplant Parmesan

Ingredients

- 1 Large Eggplant Stems and Sliced
- 1/2 C Flour
- 1/2 C Almond Milk
- 1/2 C Panko Breadcrumbs

- 2 Tablespoon Grated Parmesan
- Onion Powder to Powder taste
- Salt and pepper to taste to top the parmesan: or Parmesan for Serving
- to serve more1 c Marinara Sauce
- 1/2 c Vegan Mozzarella Shreds
- Vegan Grated
- 4 oz. Spaghetti or pasta of your choice cooked hard (about 2 ounces. Per person)
- Vegetarian Grated Parmesan Sprinkle
- Garnish for celery

Instructions

- Wash, dry and take away eggplant stems. Make slices.
- Dip the slices in the flour, then the almond milk and finally, the panko bread pieces you just mix with the vegan par man, salt, pepper, garlic, and onion powder.
- Spray lightly with oil (if desired) and place in an air fryer basket at 390 degrees for quarter-hour, flipping halfway (spray lightly on the other side).
- Alternatively, you will do this by beating the oven at 400 degrees. The cooking time can vary as the convection type of the air fryer uses the cooking method. Just keep an eye on them.

- While the eggplant is cooking, stir further and cook your pasta.
- When golden on each side, spoon several marinas and top with a mixture of 2 vegan cheese. Cook until the cheese begins to melt.
- Serve with pasta (and extra sauce), garnishing with fresh parsley and perhaps another sprinkle of vegetarian parmesan. Enjoy it!

Crispy Baked Artichoke Fries

Ingredients

- 1 cup all-purpose flour
- 1/2 - 1 cup vegetable-based milk (I used almonds)
- 1/2 teaspoon garlic powder
- 3/4 teaspoon salt

- 1/4 tsp black pepper, to taste for a mixer dry
- 1 1/2 cups pancake breadcrumbs
- 1/2 tsp paprika
- 1/4 tsp salt

Instructions

- If you are using an oven, put it at 500F Preheat. Then, remove the can of artichoke hurts and cut them into quarters.
- Place quarter artichoke hearts on one half and clean tea towel during a row. Fold the opposite half towel over the top of the quarter and press gently to get rid of the moisture. When you are preparing the wet and dry mix, allow the artichoke to sit inside the towel.
- Prepare the weight mix by putting all the ingredients in a small bowl with a wide rim. I suggest starting with 1/2 cup of plant milk and behaving your high in 1 tbsp increase. You will want the combination to be slightly thicker than the batter.
- Prepare a dry mix during a small bowl with a wide rim.
- Using different hands for each mix, dip each artichoke quarter into the weight mix, gently shake the surplus batter, then pour it into the dry mix and coat well. Repeat with all artichoke pieces.
- To bake artichoke fries

- In the oven: Place on a greased or lined baking sheet and bake at 500F for 10-13 minutes
- In an air fryer: Bake at 340 F for 10-13 minutes. I baked my fries in 2 batches, so there was some "breathing room" between the fries and they did not stick together.
- Serve hot and with any dipping sauce of your choice.

Note:

You can use any flour for a weighted mix, but every flour absorbs a specific amount of liquid. I can suggest starting with 1/2 cup of plant milk and treat your high in 1 tbsp increments. You will want the combination to be slightly thicker than the batter.

Some Panko Breadcrumbs are not vegetarian, so double-check the ingredients before you buy! I used some from Whole Foods, which were also free of oil.

This recipe is often made gluten-free with GF flour and breadcrumbs!

Vegetarian Corn Fritters

Ingredients

- Fresh Frozen or Grilled Whole Corn Kernels About 2Finely Grilled
- Corn + 2-3 Karachi Almond Milk Plus Salt "For Creamed Corn Blend" / 1 cc of Pepper, for Taste
- 1/3 Cornmeal

- 1/3 c flour
- 1/2 teaspoon yeast
- onion Powder Wad
- garlic powder Shake
- 1/4 teaspoon paprika
- Rake with 2 table green peppers
- about 1/4 c chopped Italian parsley
- Live Nest frying Oil
- The tangy dipping sauce: to
- 4 tbsp vegetarian mayonnaise
- 2 grainy mustard spoon or Swaddle

Instructions

- Dry ingredients (flour with whisk cornmeal, leaven, seasonings, and parsley).
- In a kitchen appliance, 1 tablespoon of corn with 2-3 tablespoons of almond milk. Season with salt and pepper.
- Add corn mixture to flour mixture until well mixed.
- Add two seas of whole corn kernels, folded to the mixture. Do not finish the work and do not add more flour or cornmeal. It will seem loose but will be arranged as soon as they cook.
- Heat a pan on medium-high heat then add about 1 tbsp of oil.

- Using a cookie scoop, firmly place the batter in the pan. Employing a spatula, it quickly flattens to form a patty shape.
- Allow to cook until one side is golden and flip the opposite side to cook.
- Remove paper to get rid of any excess oil. Season with salt.
- Stir the ingredients of the dipping sauce together and serve immediately.

Vegan Bacon-Wrapped Mini Breakfast Burritos

Ingredients

- 2 tablespoons cashew butter
- 2 - 3 tablespoons Tamari
- 1 - 2 tablespoons of liquid smoke
- 1-2 tablespoons water tablespoons
- 4 paper
- 4 serving swages as scrambled or tofu scrambled veggies
- 1/3 cup roasted.
- 8 strips roasted red chili

- 1 small tree broccoli,
- 6-8 stalks fresh asparagus
- handful spinach, kale, other greens

Instructions

- Preheat the oven to 350 ° F. Line the baking sheet with parchment paper.
- In a small shallow bowl, mix cashew butter, tamari, liquid smoke, and water.
- Prepare all the filler to assemble the rolls.
- Rice Paper Hydrating Technique: Able to fill/roll an outer plate/surface. Hold a paper under cold water running from the tap water, wetting each side of the wrapper, for only a few seconds. Remove from the water and while still firm, place it on a plate to fill - the paper will soften as it sits, but will not be so soft that it sticks to the surface or is handled.
- Fill with paper, leaving only the sides, keeping the contents away from the center. Fold two sides like a burrito, roll from component side to another side, and seal. Dip each roll in cashews - liquid smoke mixture, coating completely. Arrange the rolls on a parchment baking sheet.
- Bake at 350 ° F for a quarter of an hour. Remove from the oven, turn, return and continue baking for an additional 10 minutes until the bacon is crispy. Serve hot

Meatless Monday Air Fryer Thai Veggie Bites

Ingredients

- 1 large broccoli
- 1 large cauliflower
- 6 large carrot
- handful of peas
- cauliflower made in rice "
- large onions peeled and dried
- 1 small powder
- 2 leeks cleaned and finely chopped shrimp
- 1 coconut Can be taken in milk.

- 50 gems to 1 cm cube ginger peeled and grated
- 1 tablespoon garlic puree
- 1 tablespoon vegetable oil
- 1 tbsp Thai green curry paste
- 1 tablespoon coriander
- 1 tablespoon
- mix 1 teaspoon cumin
- salt and pepper
- Metric - Imperial

Instructions

- Garlic in a pan, Cook your onion with ginger and onion. Vegetable oil until the onion has a nice bit of color.
- While you are cooking your onions, cook your vegetables (other than the courtyard and the leek) for 20 minutes or until almost cooked.
- Add the agate, leeks and hence curry paste to your pan and cook for 5 minutes on medium heat.
- Add coconut milk and so mix the remaining portion of the spice mixture well, then add cabbage rice.
- Mix again and let simmer for 10 minutes.
- Once it boils for 10 minutes and so the sauce has reduced by half, add boiled vegetables. Mix well and you will now have a surprise base for your veggie bytes.
- Keep in the refrigerator for an hour to chill.

- Make bite-sized pieces and place them in the air fryer after one hour. Cook for 10 minutes at 180c then serves as it cools.

Notes:

For the best results, cover your hands in flour and as you cut the veggies, they are going to take in the flour and make a better combination. Also, keep the cutting on the baking sheet in your air fryer to make it worse later.

Classic Falafel

Ingredients

- 1 ½ cup dry garbanzo beans
- ½ cup chopped fresh parsley
- ½ cup chopped fresh coriander
- ½ cup chopped white onion
- 7 cloves garlic
- 2 Karachi. All-purpose flour

- Small spoon. Sea salt
- 1 tbsp. ground cumin
- . Small spoon. Ground cardamom
- 1 tsp. Ground
- coriander. Small spoon. Red chili

Instructions

- Soak them overnight: Place dried garbanzo beans during the canopy with a large bowl and 1 inch of water. Let sit for 20-24 hours. Drain well. Quick soak: Rinse garbanzo beans during a sieve and raises an outer pot. Cover with 2 inches of water and bring to a boil. Allow boiling for 1 minute, cover the pot and take it away from heat. Represent 1 hour. Drain well.
- In a kitchen appliance bowl, add parsley, cilantro, onion, and garlic. Stir until well mixed.
- Add soaked garbanzo beans, flour, salt, cumin, cardamom, coriander and cayenne to the kitchen appliance. Pulse until the material forms a course, coarse meal. Sometimes scrape the edges of the kitchen appliance.
- Place the mixture in a bowl, cool the flavors to cover and return together for 1-2 hours.
- Once cooled, remove from the refrigerator and make 1-inch inch balls, then flatten the balls a little.

- Heat the air to 400 degrees Fahrenheit. Lightly spray the fryer basket with oil.
- Place falafel in a basket, so that there is no overcrowding. Cook for 10 minutes, turning halfway through. Repeat with the remaining falafel.

Chapter 5: Air Fried Mediterranean Lunch Recipes

Air Fryer Fish and Fries

Ingredients

- 1-pound potato (about 2 medium)
- 2 tablespoons vegetable oil
- 1/4 teaspoon pepper
- 1/4 teaspoon salt

- Fish
- 1/3 cup all-purpose flour
- 1/4 teaspoon pepper
- 2 large eggs
- 2 tablespoons water
- 2/3 cup crushed cornflakes
- 1 tablespoon grated Parmesan cheese
- 1/8 teaspoon cayenne pepper
- 1/4 teaspoon salt
- 1-pound haddock or cod filters
- tartar sauce, alternate

Instructions

- Preheat the air fryer at 400 °. Peel and cut potatoes into 1/2-inch-thick slices; cut the slices into 1/2-in-thick sticks.
- In a large bowl, add potatoes with oil, pepper, and salt. Working in batches as needed, place potatoes during one layer in an air-fryer basket; Cook only until tender, 5–10 minutes to re-divide potatoes in baskets; Still light brown and crisp, cook for 5–10 minutes.
- Meanwhile, during a shallow bowl, mix flour and pepper. In another shallow bowl, whisk the egg with water. During a third bowl, toss corn flakes with cheese and cayenne. Sprinkle fish with salt; Dough mixture to read both sides;

Stir excess. Dip in egg mixture, then in the cornflake mixture, pat to aid adherence to coat.

- Remove the fries from the basket; To keep safe. Place the fish in a single layer in the fryer basket. Cook until the fish turns light brown and just starts to flourish easily with a fork, turning halfway through cooking. Do not overcook. Return the fries to heat through the basket. Serve immediately. If desired, serve with spicy chutney.

Cheese Egg Rolls

Ingredients

- 1/2-pound bulk sausage
- 1/2 cup chopped tart cheddar
- 1/2 cup chopped Monterey Jack cheese
- 1 tbsp chopped green onion

- 1 tbsp 2% milk
- 1/4 tsp salt
- 1/8 teaspoon black pepper
- 1 tablespoon butter
- 12 spring roll wrappers
- maple syrup or salsa, alternate

Instructions

- In a small nonstick pan, cooks the sausage over medium heat until it becomes pink, 4-6 minutes, breaking into pieces; drain. Stir in cheeses and green onions; put aside. Clean and wipe.
- In a small bowl, whisk eggs, milk, salt, and pepper. Within the same pan, heat the butter over medium heat. Pour in egg mixture; Cook and shake until the eggs thicken and no liquid egg remains. Stir in the sausage mixture.
- Preheat the air fryer at 400 degrees. With one corner of a spring roll wrapper, you place 1/4 cup slightly below the center of the wrapper. (Cover the remaining wrapper with a damp towel until able to use.) Fold the bottom corner over the filling; Moisten the remaining cover edges with water. Fold corners toward the center on filling. Roll the spring tightly, press on the tip to seal. Repeat
- In batches, arrange egg rolls during a crust on an increased tray in an air-fryer basket, Sprites with cooking spray.

Cook for 3-4 minutes until it becomes light brown. Turn, Sprites with cooking spray. Cook for 3-4 minutes until golden brown and crisp. Serve with syrup or salsa if desired.

Air Fryer Shrimp

Ingredients

- 1/2 cup mayonnaise
- 1 tbsp creole mustard
- 1 tbsp chopped cornichons or dill pickles
- 1 tbsp minced boiled
- 1/8 teaspoon cayenne pepper
- Coconut Shrimp

- 1 cup all-flour
- 1 teaspoon Herbs de Provence
- 1/2 teaspoon sea salt
- 1/2 teaspoon garlic powder
- 1/2 teaspoon pepper
- 1/4 teaspoon pepper black pepper
- 1 large egg
- 1/2 cup 2% milk
- 1 teaspoon hot onion
- cups sweetened shredded Nair Ripe.
- 1 pound uncooked (avid per pound), peeled and cooked hoagie
- cooking spray
- 4 buns,
- 2 cups of chopped lettuce
- 1 medium tomato, finely chopped

Instructions

- For remoulade, during a small bowl, add primary ingredients, Mix. Refrigerate, cover, serve until.
- Preheat the air fryer to 375 °. During a shallow bowl, mix flour, herbs de Provence, sea salt, garlic powder, black pepper, and cayenne. Whisk egg, milk, and warm poised during a separate shallow bowl. Place the coconut during the third shallow bowl. Dip the shrimp in flour to coat both

sides; Stir excess. Dip in egg mixture, then in coconut, pat to adhere.
- In batches, arrange the shrimp during one layer in an enlarged air-fryer basket; Sprites with cooking spray. Cook until the coconut turns light brown and the shrimp turns pink, 3-4 minutes on all sides.
- Spread the cut side of the buns with remoulade. Top with shrimp, lettuce and tomatoes.

Air Fryer Nashville Hot Chicken

Ingredients

- 2 tablespoons pickle juice, split, split
- 2 tablespoons hot plover peppers
- 1 teaspoon salt,
- 2 pounds chicken tenderloin
- 1 cup all-flour
- 1/2 teaspoon pepper 1/2
- 1 Large egg
- Half cup buttermilk

- Cooking Spray
- 1/2 cup vegetable oil
- 2 tablespoons cayenne pepper
- 2 tbsp dark sugar
- 1 teaspoon paprika
- 1 teaspoon flavor
- 1/2 teaspoon garlic powder
- Dill pickle slices

Instructions

- In a bowl or shallow dish, 1 tbsp Pickle juice, 1 tbsp sauce, and 1/2 teaspoon combine salt. Add chicken and switch to coat. Refrigerate, cover, minimum of 1 hour. Drain, discard pickles of any kind.
- Preheat the air fryer to 375 °. During a shallow bowl, mix flour, remaining 1/2 teaspoon salt and pepper. In another shallow bowl, whisk eggs, buttermilk, remaining 1 tbsp pickle juice and 1 tbsp sauce. To coat both sides of the chicken in flour; Stir excess. Dip in egg mixture, but flour mixture.
- In batches, arrange the chicken during a crust on a well-grown tray in an air-fryer basket, Sprites with cooking spray. Cook until golden brown, 5-6 minutes. Turn, Sprites with cooking spray. Cook for 5-6 minutes, until golden brown.

- Oil, cayenne pepper, sugar, and spice together; Pour hot chicken and toss to coat. Serve with Pickle

Air Fryer Crispy Spring Rolls

Ingredients

- 3 cups coleslaw mix (about 7 ounces)
- 3 green onions, chopped
- 1 tbsp soy
- 1 tablespoon vegetable oil
- 1-pound boneless chicken breasts

- skinless tsp flavor
- 2 packages (8 ounces each) cheese, softened
- 2 tablespoons) Sriracha Masala
- 24 egg roll wrappers
- cooking spray
- sweet masala, optional

Instructions

- Preheat the air fryer at 360 degrees. Toss Coleslaw mixture, green onion, soy and sesame oil; Stand while making chicken. Place the chicken in an increased air-fryer basket during a crust. Cook the thermometer inserted in the chicken for 165 °, 18-20 minutes. Remove Chicken; Little cool. Finely chopped chicken; Toss with flavor.
- Raise the air fryer temperature to 400 °. During a large bowl, combine cheese and Sriracha chili sauce; Stir in the chicken and coleslaw mixture. With one corner of the egg roll wrapper facing you, fill about 2 tablespoons under the center of the wrapper. (Cover the remaining wrapper with a damp towel until able to use.) Fold the bottom corner over the filling; Moisten the remaining edges with water. Fold corners toward the center on filling; Roll tightly, press the tip to seal. Repeat
- In batches, arrange spring rolls during one layer in an enlarged air-fryer basket; Sprites with cooking spray. Cook

until light brown, 5-6 minutes. Turn, Sprites with cooking spray. Cook for 5-6 minutes, until golden brown and crisp. If desired, serve with sweet spices.

- Freeze option: Freeze spring roll 1 of the freeze. Also, in freezer containers, separate the layers with wax paper. To use, cook frozen spring rolls as directed, extending time as needed.

Air Fryer Beef Swiss Bundles

Ingredients

- 1-pound hamburger
- 1/2 cups chopped fresh mushrooms
- 1/2 cup chopped onion
- 1/2 teaspoon minced garlic crushed
- 4 teaspoon Worcester sauce
- 3/4 teaspoon dried rosemary, Happened.
- 3/4 teaspoon paprika
- 1/2 teaspoon salt
- 1/4 teaspoon pepper
- 1 sheet frozen puff pastry, melted

- 2/3 cup refrigerated mashed potatoes
- 1 cup chopped swiss
- 2 tbsp water

Instructions

- Air from 375 ° Preheat Arya. During a large skillet, cook beef, mushrooms, and onions over medium heat until the meat is no longer pink, and the vegetables are tender, 8–10 minutes. Add garlic; cook 1 minute more. Stir in Worcester sauce and seasonings. Remove from heat; put aside.
- On a lightly puffed surface, roll the puff pastry 15x13-inches. Rectangle. Dig four 7-1 / 2x6-1 / 2-inch. Rectangles. Place about 2 tablespoons of potatoes over each rectangle; Spread to 1 of the edges. Top each with 3/4 cup beef mixture; sprinkle with 1/4 cup cheese.
- Beat egg and water; Brush some on the pastry edges. Bring opposite corners of the pastry above each bundle; Sew pinch to seal. Brush with the remaining egg mixture.
- In batches, place pastry during a single layer in an air-fryer basket; Cook for 10-12 minutes until golden brown.
- Freeze option: Stab the unbaked pastry on a parchment-lined baking sheet. Transfer to an airtight container; Return to the freezer. To use, direct the frozen pastry until

golden brown and warm it by increasing the time to 15-20 minutes.

Air Fryer Wasabi Crab

Ingredients

- 1 medium sweet red chili, finely chopped
- 1 celery rib, finely chopped
- 3 green onions, finely chopped
- 2 large egg whites
- 3 tablespoons low-fat mayonnaise
- 1/4 teaspoon prepared wasabi
- 1 / 4 teaspoons salt
- 1 /. 3 cups plus 1/2 cup dry breadcrumbs,

- 1/2 cups lump crab, dried
- Cooking spray

Sauce:

- 1 celery rib, sliced
- 1/3 cup low-fat mayonnaise
- 1 scallion, sliced
- 1 tablespoon pickle Troilus
- prepare the wasabi prepared by 1/2 teaspoon
- 1/4 teaspoon, preheat the

Instructions

- 375 degrees to fry. Spirit fryer basket with cooking spray. Combine the first 7 ingredients; add 1/3 cup breadcrumbs. Fold gently into the crab.
- Keep the remaining breadcrumbs during a shallow bowl. Spoon heaping crab mixture into the cramp. Gently coat and shape into a 3/4-inch-thick patty. Working in batches as needed, place the crab cakes during one layer in the basket. Spirit Crab Cake with Cooking Spray. Cook for 8–12 minutes until golden brown, carefully closing the cooking halfway point and spraying with additional cooking spray. Remove and keep warm. Repeat with remaining crab cakes.

- Meanwhile, place the sauce ingredients in the food processor; 2 or 3 times to mix the pulse or until the desired consistency is reached. Serve dip cake immediately with sauce.

Air Fryer Hamburger Wellington

Ingredients

- 1/2 cup chopped fresh mushrooms
- 1 tbsp butter
- 2 tablespoons all-purpose flour

- 1/4 teaspoon pepper, split
- 1/2 cup half and half cream
- 2 tbsp finely chopped onions
- 1/4 teaspoon salt
- 1/2-pound hamburger
- 1 tube (4 ounces) refrigerated crescent rolls
- 1 large egg, lightly beaten, optional
- 1 teaspoon flakes dried parsley

Instructions

- Preheat air300 degrees, Fryer. While in a saucepan, heat the butter over medium-high heat. Add mushrooms; cook and stir until tender, 5-6 minutes. Stir in the flour and 1/8 teaspoon pepper until mixed. Apply the cream slowly. Bring back a boil; cook and stir for two minutes or until thickened. Remove from heat and keep aside.
- In a bowl, combine ingredients, onion, 2 tablespoons sauce, salt and remaining 1/8 teaspoon pepper. Mixture and mix well-lacking beef. Shape into 2 loaves. Separate the crescent dough into 2 rectangles: Press holes to seal. Place meat bread on each rectangle. Bring the edges together and pinch to seal. If desired, brush with beaten egg.

- Place the Wellington in an enlarged air-fryer basket during a crust. Cook until golden brown and a thermometer inserted into the meatloaf reads 160 °, 18–22 minutes.
- Meanwhile, heat remaining sauce over low heat; Stir in parsley. Serve sauce with Wellington.

Air Fryer Loaded Pork Burritos

Ingredients

- 3/4 cup molten lime concentrate
- 1 tbsp vegetable oil
- 2 tablespoons salt
- 1/2 tablespoons pepper split divided
- 1-1/2 pounds of pork into the bonnet, thin strips
- 1 cup chopped seeds chopped. Plum tomatoes
- 1 small sweet chili,

- 1 small onion chopped,
- 1/4 cup plus 1/3 cup minced fresh
- 1 jalapeno, seeds and sliced uncooked
- 1 tbsp juice
- 1/4 teaspoon powder
- 1 cup of rice
- 2 cups of sliced Monterey Jack Cheese
- 6 flour tortillas (12 in), hot
- 1 can (15 oz) black beans, rinsed and drained
- 1/2 cups sour cream
- cooking spray

Instructions

- Limed concentrate, in a large shallow dish Oil, 1 combine teaspoon salt and 1/2 teaspoon pepper; add pork. Address quote: Cover and refrigerate for at least 20 minutes.
- For salsa, during a small bowl, combine tomatoes, sweet peppers, onions, 1/4 cup ditophal, jalapeno, juice, garlic powder, and the remaining salt and pepper.
- Meanwhile, cook rice as per package instructions. Stir in the remaining cilantro; To keep safe.
- Drain pork, discard pickles. Preheat the air fryer to 350 degrees in batches and place pork in a single air-fryer basket during a single layer; Sprites with cooking spray. Cook until the pork is pink, 8-10 minutes, turning halfway.

- Sprinkle 1/3 cup of cheese off-center on each tortilla. Mix each with 1/4 cup salsa, 1/2 cup rice mixture, 1/4 cup black beans and 1/4 cup sour cream, about 1/2 cup pork. Fill the sides and ends on the filling. Serve with the remaining salsa.

Air Fryer Green Tomato

Ingredients

- 2 medium green tomatoes (about 10 ounces)
- 1/2 teaspoon salt
- 1/4 teaspoon pepper

- 1 large egg, beaten
- 1/4 cup all-purpose flour
- 1 cup panko breadcrumbs
- Cooking spray
- 1 / 2 cups low-fat mayonnaise
- 2 green onions, finely chopped
- 1 teaspoon fresh dill or 1/4 teaspoon dilute,
- 8 slices toasted whole wheat bread
- 8 cooked centers cut bacon strips
- 4 Bibb or Boston salad leaves

Instructions

- 350 Preheat air Fryer °. Cut each tomato bowl into 4 slices. Sprinkle it with salt and pepper. Put eggs, flour, and breadcrumbs in separate shallow bowls. Dip the tomato slices in the flour, shaking off the excess, then read the eggs, and finally tap into the bread crumb mixture to adhere.
- In batches, arrange tomato slices during a crust on an increased tray in an air-fryer basket, Sprites with cooking spray. Cook for 4-6 minutes until golden brown. Turn, Sprites with cooking spray. Cook for 4-6 minutes until golden brown.
- Meanwhile, combine mayonnaise, green onion, and dill. Layer each of the 4 slices of bread with 2 bacon strips, 1

salad leaf and a couple of tomato slices. Spread mayonnaise mixture over remaining slices of bread, Place from above. serve immediately.

Air Fryer Tortellini with Prosciutto

Ingredients

- 1 tablespoon vegetable oil
- 3 tablespoons finely chopped onion
- 4 garlic cloves, coarsely chopped
- 1 can (15 ounces) tomato puree
- 1 tbsp minced fresh basil

- 1/4 teaspoon salt
- 1 / 4 teaspoon pepper
- Tortellini:
- 2 large eggs
- 2 tablespoons 2% milk
- 2/3 cup spice breadcrumbs
- 1 teaspoon garlic powder
- 2 tablespoons grated Pecorino Romano cheese
- 1 tablespoon fresh parsley
- 1/2 teaspoon salt
- 1 packaging (12 ounces) refrigerated Prosciutto Ricotta Tortellini
- cooking spray

Instructions

- Heat in a small saucepan. Oil over medium-high heat. Add onion and garlic; cook and stir until tender, 3-4 minutes. Stir in tomato puree, basil, salt, and pepper. Bring back a boil; warm down. Simmer, open, 10 minutes. To keep safe.
- Meanwhile, preheat the air fryer to 350 °. During a small bowl, egg, and milk. In another bowl, combine breadcrumbs, garlic powder, cottage cheese, parsley, and salt.
- Dip the Angelina in the egg mixture, then coat it in the bread crumb mixture. In batches, arrange tortellini during

one layer in an enlarged air-fryer basket; Sprites with cooking spray. Cook 4-5 minutes until golden brown. Turn, Sprites with cooking spray. Cook for 4-5 minutes, until golden brown. Serve with Sauce, Sprinkle with additional minced fresh basil.

Air Fryer Herb and Cheese-Stuffed Burger

Ingredients

- 2 green onions, finely chopped
- 2 tablespoons fresh parsley
- 4 tablespoons mustard,
- daejon3 tablespoons dry breadcrumbs
- 2 tablespoons ketchup

- 1/2 teaspoon salt
- 1/2 teaspoon dried Henna, crushed Hochmuth.
- 14 teaspoon dried sage leaves
- 1-pound lean hamburger (90% lean)
- 2 ounces cheddar, sliced
- 4 hamburger buns, split
- Optional toppings: lettuce, sliced tomatoes, mayonnaise, and extra ketchup

Instructions

- Air Fryer preheat to 375 °. During a small bowl, combine a pair of green onions, parsley and a tablespoon of mustard. In another bowl, add breadcrumbs, ketchup, seasonings and the remaining 2 tablespoons of mustard. Add beef to the bread crumb mixture; mix lightly but well.
- Shape mixture into 8 thin patties. Place sliced cheese in the center of 4 patties; Spoon mixture over cheese. Top with the remaining patties, taking care to seal them completely, pressing the edges firmly.
- Place the burger during a crust in an air-fryer basket. Working in batches as required, air-fry 8 minutes; flip and continue cooking until the thermometer reads 160 °, 6-8 minutes longer. Serve burgers on buns with toppings if desired.

Air Fryer Turkey Croquettes

Ingredients

- 2 cups mashed potatoes (with added milk and butter)
- 1/2 cup grated cheese
- 1/2 cup chopped Swiss cheese
- 1 onion, finely chopped

- 2 tablespoons minced fresh henna or 1/2 teaspoon dry henna, crushed
- 1 teaspoon minced fresh sage or 1/4 teaspoon dried sage leaves
- 1/2 teaspoon salt
- 1/4 teaspoon pepper
- 3 cups finely chopped cooked turkey
- 2 tbsp water
- 1 -1 / 4 Panko Bread Crumb This
- Butter-Flavor Cooking Spray
- Sour. Cream, alternate

Instructions

- Heat the air floor to 350 °. During a large bowl, combine the mashed potatoes, cottage cheese, shallot, rosemary, sage, salt, and pepper; Stir in turkey. Twelve 1-in.-thick patties in size.
- In a shallow bowl, whisk eggs and water. Place the breadcrumbs in another shallow bowl. Dip the crisps in the egg mixture, then pat in the breadcrumbs to aid adherence to the coating.
- In batches, place croquettes during a single layer in a Greer fryer basket; Sprites with cooking spray. Cook 4-5 minutes until golden brown. Turn, Sprites with cooking spray.

Cook until golden brown; 4-5 minutes. If desired, serve with sour cream.

Air Fryer Bourbon Bacon Cinnamon Rolls

Ingredients

- 8 bacon strips
- 3/4 cup bourbon
- 1 tube (12.4 oz) refrigerated cinnamon rolls
- 1/2 cup chopped pecans
- 2 tablespoons syrup
- 1 tablespoon minced fresh ginger root

Instructions

- Place bacon during shallow dish; Add bourbon. Seal and refrigerate overnight. Remove bacon and pat dry; Discard the burbs.
- In a large pan, baking bacon in batches over medium heat is almost crisp but still viable. Remove paper towels to empty. Discard about 1 teaspoon of drippings.
- Preheat the air fryer to 350 degrees. Separate the dough into 8 rolls, burning the icing packet. Unscrew the spiral rolls into long strips; 6x1-in to make the pat dough. Strips. Place 1 bacon on each strip of flour, trimming the bacon as needed: Formation of the spiral. Pinch ends to seal. Repeat with remaining flour. Transfer 4 rolls to the air-fryer basket; Cook for 5 minutes. Turn the rolls over and cook for about 4 minutes until they turn golden brown.
- Meanwhile, mix pecans and syrup. In another bowl, shake the ginger with the contents of the icing packet. In the same pan, heat remaining bacon dripping over medium heat. Add pecan mixture; Cook, frequently stirring until lightly fry, 2-3 minutes.
- Drizzle half the pieces on a hot cinnamon roll; Top with half the pecans. Repeat to make a second batch.

Air Fryer Coconut Shrimp and Sauce

Ingredients

- 1/2 pounds Large Shrimp
- 1/2 Cups Sweet Sliced Coconut
- 1/2 cup Panko Breadcrumbs
- 4 Large Egg Whites

- Dashes Louisiana-Style Sauce
- 1/4 Spoon Salt
- 1/4 teaspoon pepper
- 1/2 cup all-purpose flour

Instructions

- Preheat the air 375 ° Fryer. Peel and Devin are leaving the shrimp on the tail.
- In a shallow bowl, toss the coconut with the breadcrumbs. In another shallow bowl, whisk egg whites, hot sauce, salt, and pepper. Place the dough during the third shallow bowl.
- To lightly coat shrimp in flour; Stir excess. Dip in albumen mixture, then in coconut mixture, pat to aid adherence of coating.
- Spray the fryer basket with cooking spray. Working in batches as needed, place the shrimp in the basket during a single layer. Cook for 4 minutes; Turn the shrimp on and continue cooking until the coconut turns light brown and the shrimp turns pink another 4 minutes.
- Meanwhile, combine sauce ingredients during a small saucepan; Cook and shake over medium-low heat until preserved. Serve shrimp immediately with chutney.

Air Fryer Quentin-Bourbon Feather

Ingredients

- 1/2 cup peach retains
- 1 tbsp sugar
- 1 garlic clove, minced
- 1/4 tsp salt
- 2 tbsp white vinegar
- 2 tbsp bourbon
- 1 tsp cornstarch

- 1/2 tablespoons water
- pounds of chicken wings

Instructions

- Preheat the air fryer at 400 degrees. Preserve sugar, garlic and salt during the food processor, process until blended. Transfer to a little saucepan. Add vinegar and bourbon; Bring back a boil. Warm down; Boil, uncovered, until slightly thickened, 4-6 minutes.
- In a small bowl, mix cornstarch and water until smooth; Stir in the preserved mixture. Return to a boil, stirring constantly; Cook for 1-2 minutes or until thickened. Reserve 1/4 cup sauce for serving.
- Using a sharp knife, cut back 2 joints on each chicken wing: Discard wing tips. Spray the air fryer basket with cooking spray. Working in batches as needed, place the wing pieces during one layer in the air fryer basket. Cook for 6 minutes; turn and brush with preserved mixture. Return to the air fryer and cook until it turns brown and the juices run clear for 6-8 minutes. Remove and keep warm. Repeat with the remaining wing pieces. Serve the wings immediately with reserved chutney.

Chapter 6: Air Fried Mediterranean Snack Recipes

Air Fryer Pizza

Ingredients

- Buffalo Mozzarella
- Pizza Dough 1 12 Inch Dough Will Make 2 Individual Size Pizza
- Olive Oil
- Tomato Sauce

- Optional Topping: Fresh Basil, Parmesan Cheese, Pepper Seeds to Finish

Instructions

- Prep: Preheat air fryer to 375 ° F (190 ° C)). Thoroughly spray the air fryer basket with oil. Pat mozzarella dries with paper towels (to prevent a disgusting pizza).
- Assemble: Roll the pizza dough to the dimensions of your air fryer basket. Carefully transfer it to the air fryer, then brush it lightly with about a teaspoon of vegetable oil. Spoon over a light layer of spaghetti sauce and sprinkle with a slice of buffalo mozzarella.
- Bake: for about 7 minutes until the crust is crispy and the cheese is melted. Alternately top with basil, grated Parmesan, and pepper flakes before serving.

Air Fried Vegetables

Ingredients

- Tender Vegetables
- Crucifers Broccoli, Cauliflower, Brussels Sprouts Like
- Capsicum, Veggies, Tomato
- Asparagus LinkedIn
- Firm Vegetables
- Root Vegetable Carrots, Beets, Potatoes, Beet
- Winter Squash Butternut, Acorn, Pumpkin
- Frozen vegetables

Instructions

- 375 degrees F (190 C) to preheat the air fryer to tender Sibson Jiu. Veggies by chopping them to your preferred dimensions, alternately dripping with oil (this will give them a more frying edge within the end Will taste) Raise your air fryer in as flat of a layer as possible and cook for 10 to fifteen minutes, cooking in the market even while shaking the air fryer pan once or twice while cooking.
- Firm veggie: 375 degrees F (190 C) to preheat air fryer. Prepare them by cutting them to your preferred dimensions (remember small pieces cook faster!) Dripping alternately with oil and raising your air fryer in as flat of a layer as possible. Cook for 20 to half an hour, keep the air fryer pan shaking for some time while cooking, even for cooking.
- Frozen Vegetables: Find out which category your vegetable falls under (see tender or firm, see the note above), then add a few minutes to the cooking time to account for the melting vegetables during the cooking process. Make sure they offer space between your vegetables to be fully roasted.

Baked General Tso's Cauliflower

Ingredients

- Cauliflower
- Half-Head Cauliflower
- Half-Cup Dough
- 2 Large Eggs

- 60gTransported 1 Cup Panko Breadcrumbs 50g15ml
- ¼ Spoon Each Salt and Pepper
- General Tso's Sauce
- 1 Gourd Vegetable Oil
- 2 Cloves Garlic Minced
- 1 Gourd Fresh grated ginger
- ½ cup vegetable broth 120 mL
- soy cup soy 60 mL
- vine cup rice vinegar 60 mL
- sugar cup sugar 50 grams
- 2 tons 2 tablespoons 30
- tablespoons cornstarch 2 tablespoons (30 mA) L) 15 gin cold water

Instructions

- Prep: 400 ° F (204) ° C in a preheated oven) *. Arrange the workspace by placing flour, egg, and panko in separate bowls. Add salt and pepper to the poncho. Cut the cabbage into bite-sized flowers.
- Dredge: Working in batches, coat the florets in flour, then egg, then breadcrumbs. Combine parchment paper-lined baking sheets. Bake for 15 to 20 minutes, or until crispy.
- Sauce: Set a little saucepan over medium heat and add vegetable oil, garlic, and ginger. Cook two minutes until fragrant, then add the remaining sauce ingredients,

leaving the cornstarch mixture. Mix and boil. While whisking, slowly pour within the cornstarch mixture. It should thicken quite quickly; If not, keep boiling until thick.
- Assemble: Drizzle sauce over the cooked cabbage and toss gently to coat evenly. Serve cauliflower over hot rice or quinoa.

Crispy Baked Avocado Tacos

Ingredients

- 1 cup finely chopped or crushed pineapple 240 grams
- Romana 1 tomato finely chopped
- 1/2 red pepper, finely chopped
- 1/2 medium Purple onion 1/2 cup, finely. Chopped

- 1 clove minced garlic
- 1/2 jalapeno finely chopped
- pinch of cumin and salt
- avocado tacos
- 1 advocator
- 1/4 cup alate 35 grams
- 1 large egg
- whipped 1/2 cup pence crabs 65 grams
- pinch each salt and black Chili
- 4 Maida Tortilla Click for recipe
- Adobo Sauce
- 1/4 cup plain yogurt 60 grams
- 2 Karachi mayonnaise 30 grams
- 1/4 teaspoon juice
- Chipotle pepper 1 Karachi adobo sauce from a jar

Instructions

- Salsa: All Salsa Ingredients (Patel Combine processor sliced by hand or blitz within the food), cover, and set in the fridge.
- Prep Avocado: Cut the avocado in half lengthwise and remove the pit. Put the avocado skin down and cut each half into 4 equal size pieces, then gently peel off the skin.
- Prep Station: Preheat oven to 450 F (230 C) or 375 F (190 C) to air fryer. Arrange your workspace so that you get a

bowl of flour, a bowl of whisked eggs, a bowl of Panko with S&P and a parchment-lined baking sheet on top.
- Coat: Dip each piece of avocado first within the flour, then egg, then panko. Place on a prepared baking sheet and bake or air fry for 10 minutes, half-cooked until lightly cooked.
- Sauce: While the avocados are cooking, mix all the sauce ingredients.
- Serve: Spoon salsa on a tortilla, drizzle with 2 pieces of avocado and sauce. Serve immediately and enjoy!

Baked Potatoes

Instructions

- Cake Air Fryer Prep: Preheat air fryer to 390 degrees F (200 C). Rub the potatoes with a little oil and sprinkle with salt.
- Cook: Set the potatoes within the air fryer during the same layer. Cook for 30 to 45 minutes, or until fork-tender, flip them once while cooking to cook evenly.
- air fryer french-fried potatoes
- Soak the: With the help of a matchstick or knife, break the potato or cut it into a mandolin slicer. Soak sliced potatoes in a bowl of cold water for 1 to 2 hours. This

removes the starch to offer them a completely crispy texture!

- Prep: Preheat air fryer to 390 degrees F (200 C). Dry and pat dry potatoes. Increase a bowl, then drizzle with oil (about 1 teaspoon per potato) and a pinch of salt.
- Cook: Add fries to your air fryer, opened as crusted as possible. Cook for 15 to twenty minutes, stirring the basket once or twice while cooking evenly.

Air Fryer Potato Chips

Instructions

- Cut the potatoes thinly using a knife or mandolin slicer. Soak sliced potatoes in a bowl of cold water for 1 to 2 hours. With a little bit of air fryer potato fry, it removes the starch to make it completely crisp.
- Prep: Preheat the air fryer to 300 degrees F (150 C). Dry and pat dry potatoes. Increase a bowl, then drizzle with oil (about 1 teaspoon per potato) and a pinch of salt.
- Cook: Add potatoes to your air fryer, open as crust as possible. Cook for 20 to half an hour, shake the basket once or twice to cook evenly. (If you hear your chips flying

within the air fryer, you will cover them with your air fryer grill plate to keep them relatively in place.)

Buttermilk Fried Mushroom

Ingredients

- 2 Heating Cups Oyster Mushrooms
- 1 Cup Buttermilk 240 See notes for ML, vegetarian options.
- 1 1/2 cups all-purpose flour 200 grams
- 1 tsp each salt, pepper, garlic powder, onion powder, smoked paprika, cumin

Instructions

- Kettle Marinette: Preheat air to 375 degrees F (190 C). During a large bowl, clean the mushrooms with buttermilk. Marinate for quarter hours.
- Breaking: Combine flour and spices during a large bowl. Spoon mushrooms out of the buttermilk (save the buttermilk). Dip each mushroom within the flour mixture, shake off the excess flour, one more time within the buttermilk, then another time within the dough (briefly: wet> dry> wet> dry).
- Cook: Stir the rock well under your air fry pan, then place the mushrooms during a single layer, leaving space between the mushrooms. Cook for five minutes, then brush all sides with a touch of oil for browning. Continue to cook for 5 to 10 minutes until golden brown and crispy.

Chapter 7: Air Fried Mediterranean Dinner Recipes

Air Fryer Blacken Fish Tacos

Ingredients

- Fryer Blacken Fish Tacos 1 (15 oz)
- Seeds Beans, Rinsed and Drenched
- 2 Year Corn,

- 1 Tablespoon Vegetable Oil
- 1 Tablespoon Juice
- 1/2 Spoon Salt
- 1 Pound Tilapia Fillets
- Cooking Spray
- 1/4 Cup Blackening Seasoning
- 4 Corn tortillas
- 1 lime
- 1 teaspoon Louisiana style sauce (optional)

Instructions

- Preheat the oven to 400 ° F (200 ° C).
- Combine black beans, corn, olive oil, lemon juice, and salt during a bowl. Gently stir until beans and corn are evenly coated; put aside.
- Lay the fish fillet on a clean surface and pat it with paper towels. Lightly sprinkle each fillet with cooking spray and sprinkle 1/2 of black pepper over the top. Flip the faults, spray with cooking spray, and sprinkle with the remaining seasonings.
- If necessary, place the fish during a crust within the basket of the air fryer working in batches. Cook for two minutes. Flip the fish over and cook for 2 more minutes, Transfer to a plate.

- Place the bean and corn mixture in the air fryer basket and cook for 10 minutes, stirring halfway through.
- Place the fish with a mixture of corn tortilla and bean and corn. Serve with lime wedges and sauce.

Air Fryer Coconut Chicken

Ingredients

- ½ cup of canned coconut milk
- ½ cup fruit juice
- 2 tablespoons sugar
- 1 tbsp soy

- 2 tablespoons Sriracha sauce
- 1 tablespoon ground ginger
- 1-pound boneless skinless chicken breasts, digging strips
- 2 eggs
- 1 cup coconut chopped sweet
- 1 cup panko bread Pieces of
- ½ teaspoon salt
- spoon ground black pepper
- easy nonstick cooking spray

Instructions

Step 1: Take a medium-sized bowl and coconut milk in the mix Whisk, fruit juice, sugar, soy sauce, Sriracha sauce, and ginger. Add chicken strips and toss to coat. Cover with wrapping and refrigerate for 2 hours or overnight.

Step 2: Preheat an air fryer to 375 degrees F (190 degrees C).

Step 3: Whisk eggs during a bowl. In a separate bowl mix chopped coconut, panko, salt, and pepper.

Step 4: Remove chicken strips from the pickle and shake off excess. Discard the remaining pickles. Dip the chicken strips in the beaten egg, then in the coconut-panko mixture, but again in the egg mixture, and again in the coconut-panko mixture, each strip income and double coating.

Step 5: Spray the air fryer basket with cooking spray.

Step 6: Place the braided chicken strips within the air fryer basket, making sure they are not touching; Add batch if necessary.

Step 7: Cook for six minutes, beat the strips, and cook until lightly brown and toasted, 4 to six minutes more.

Air Fryer Salmon Patties

Ingredients

- 12 oz salmon minced
- 1 tbsp peeled fresh chives
- 1 tablespoon dried Parsley with 1 teaspoon finely spoon powder.

- Tablespoon all-purpose flour, or as needed,
- 1 lemon
- Cooking spray

  Aioli Dipping Sauce:
- 1/2 cup mayonnaise
- 1 teaspoon finely minced garlic
- 1/2 teaspoon fresh juice
- 2 pinch cousin seasoning papaya

Instructions

- Mayonnaise, garlic, lemon juice, and Cajun seasoning mix together during a small bowl and dip sauce until needed.
- Keep salmon, chives, parsley, garlic, and salt in a medium bowl and mix well. Add flour and mix well. Divide into 4 equal parts: Mold in patties.
- Preheat the air fryer to 350 degrees F (175 degrees C). Cut the lemon into 4 slices.
- Place slices of lemon in the bottom of the air fryer basket and salmon patties on top. Lightly spray patty with cooking spray.
- Place the basket in a preheated fryer and leave the temperature up to 275 degrees F (135 degrees C).

- Cook within the air fryer until an instant-read thermometer inserted in the middle of a patty reads 145 ° F (63 ° C), 10 to fifteen minutes. Serve with sauce.

Breaded Air Fryer Pork Chops

Ingredients

- 4 boneless, center-cut pork chops, 1-inch thick
- 1 tablespoon Cajun seasoning
- 1 cheese cup cheese and garlic-flavored croutons
- 2 eggs

Instructions

Step 1: Air fryer to 390 ° F (200 ° C).

Step 2: Place the pork chops on a plate and sew each side with Cajun masala.

Step 3: Pulse croutons during small kitchen appliances until they require fine stability, Transfer to a shallow dish. Lightly beat eggs during a separate shallow dish. Dip the pork chops into the egg, closing excess drip. Bread chopping and a plate assail in coat crouton. Mist Chop with Cooking Spray.

Step 4: Spray the basket of the air fryer with cooking spray and place the choppers inside, so as not to uproot the fryer. You will need to calculate two batches on the dimensions of your air fryer.

Step 5: Cook for five minutes. If there is a dry or powdery area, chop again with a cooking spray and add mist. Cook for another 5 minutes. Repeat with remaining chops.

Air Fryer BBQ Ribs

Ingredients

- 1 Rack
- 1 Tbsp Olive Oil
- 1 Tbsp Liquid Smoke Flavor
- 1 Tablespoon Sugar

- ½ Tablespoon Salt
- Tablespoon Pepper
- Powdered Tablespoon Garlic Powder
- ½ Tablespoons Onion Powder
- ½ Tablespoons Flavors

Instructions

Step 1: Remove the membrane from the back ribs and dry ribs with a towel. Cut the rack into 4 pieces. Combine vegetable oil and liquid smoke in a small bowl and rub each side of the ribs.

Step 2: Add sugar, salt, pepper, garlic powder, onion powder and flavor during a bowl. Season each side of the ribs liberally with the seasoning mix. Let the ribs rest for half an hour to strengthen the taste.

Step 3: Preheat an air fryer to 375 degrees F (190 degrees C).

Step 4: Place the rib bone under the air fryer basket, ensuring that they are not touching; Cook in batches if necessary.

Step 5: Cook for quarter-hours. Flip the ribs (meat-side down) and cook for 10 minutes. Remove the ribs from the air fryer and brush the ribs bone-side with 1/2 cup BBQ sauce. Place the basket inside the air fryer and cook for five minutes. Flip the ribs, brushing the meat-side with the remaining 1/2 cup of BBQ sauce; cook a further 5 minutes or until desired char is achieved.

Mexican-Style Air Fryer Stuffed Chicken Breast

Ingredients

- 4 extra-long toothpicks
- 4 teaspoons flavored
- 4 teaspoons ground cumin,
- 1 skinless, boneless pigeon breasts

- 2 teaspoons flakes
- 2 teaspoons Mexican oregano
- salt and ground black pepper to taste
- all red bell pepper, onion, into thin strips
- chopped thin strips
- 1 fresh Jalapeno, sliced into thin strips
- 2 tablespoons vegetable oil time Chon

Instructions

Step 1: Toothpicks during canopy with a small bowl and water. Allow them to soak during cooking to prevent them from burning.

Step 2: Combine 2 teaspoons of flavor and one or two teaspoons of cumin during a shallow dish.

Step 3: Preheat an air fryer to 400 ° F (200 ° C).

Step 4: Place the pigeon breast on a flat surface. Slice horizontally through the center. Use a kitchen mallet or kitchen utensil about half / 4-inch thick.

Step 5: Sprinkle each breast evenly in half with the remaining flavor, remaining cumin, chipotle flakes, parsley, salt, and pepper. Place 1/2 bell pepper, onion and jalapeno within the center of 1 breast half. Roll the chicken upside down from the taped end and use 2 toothpicks to secure. Repeat with other breasts, spices and vegetables and secure with remaining toothpicks. Drizzle with vegetable oil until evenly covered, roll each roll within the chili-cumin mixture within a shallow dish.

Step 6: Place the roll-up inside the air-fryer basket, which has a side portion of a toothpick. Set a timer for six minutes.

Step 7: Continue cooking within the air fryer until the juices run clear and an instantaneous read thermometer inserted in the middle reads at a minimum of 165 ° F (74 ° C), about 5 minutes.

Step 8: Juice evenly on roll-up before serving.

Air Fryer Beef Wellington

Ingredients

- Air fryer Grill Pan
- Knife Sharpener
- Cling Film
- Homemade Liver Pate
- Homemade Shortcrust Pastry
- Beef
- 1 Medium Beaton Egg
- Salt & Piper

Instructions

- Get your Beef Sawdust clean it with Salt and Salt in Any Weather Cut it. Pepper then seal it with cling film and keep it inside the fridge for an hour.
- Make your batch of Lever Pete and Homemade Shortcrust Pastries.
- Roll your shortcrust pastry and employ a pastry brush and round the edges with the beaten egg to make it sticky for sealing.
- Then place a thin layer of homemade peat inside the outer egg line until you see white pastry.
- Remove the cling film from the meat and place the meat on top of the peat and push it down a touch.
- Meat and, therefore, peat pastry.
- Gives the meat a chance to breathe, score the highest of the pastries in that order.
- Place the air fryer on the grill pan within the air fryer and cook for 35 minutes at 160c / 320f.
- Leave to rest for a few minutes, slice and serve with roasted potatoes.

Notes:

It is easy to pre-make pastries to save on time and, therefore, already create within the day. I do a full batch of both my pastry recipe and my peat recipe. Then whatever remains are often used later.

Then fridge them both for an hour, then they become easy to handle. If you want to cheat and make it appear as if it is puff pastry, make my shortcrust pastry, but swap dough for your dough.

Easy Air Fryer Pizza

Ingredients

- 1 Whole Wheat Patina
- 2 Tablespoon Pizza Sauce or Marinara If you don't like a thick sauce, you can make 1 tablespoon
- 1/8 cup of mozzarella cheese, sliced

- 1/8 cup of cheddar, if you only use mozzarella Flavored cheese, omit and use 1/4th cup mozzarella
- 8 slices pepperoni
- olive oil spray
- 1 teaspoon chopped parsley, for pizza garnish when it is cooled Alternative

Instructions

Standard Nerdish:

- Sauce on top of pita bread drizzle, then cheese Tar pepperoni Lod war.
- Mostly, spray the pizza with vegetable oil spray.
- Keep within an air fryer for 8 minutes at 400 degrees. Sign up on the pizza at the 6-7-minute mark to make sure it is not to your liking.
- Remove pizza from the air fryer. I used a spatula. Refrigerate before serving.

Crispy Crust:

- To have a crisper crust, spray one side of the beaten bread with vegetable oil. Keep inside the air fryer at 400 degrees for 4 minutes. It can be completely crisp from one side.
- Remove the beaten bread from the air fryer. Turn the pyre on the side, which is less crisp. This could be the side that was face-down within the air fryer.

- Drizzle all over the chutney, then load pepperoni and chopped cheese on top.
- Place the pizza back within the air fryer for 3-4 minutes until the cheese is frying. Use your judgment. This will allow you to cook the pizza for a few more minutes to succeed in its essential texture.
- Remove pizza from the air fryer. I used a spatula. Refrigerate before serving.

Quinoa Air Fried Burger

Ingredients

- 1 cup quinoa red, white or multi-colored
- 1½ cups water
- 1 tablespoon salt
- fresh pepper
- 1½ cups oatmeal or wheat breadcrumbs
- 3 eggs lightly beaten
- ¼ cup white onion minced
- ½ cup cheese broken

- ¼ cup chopped fresh chives
- salt and freshly ground pepper,
- vegetable or vegetable oil
- 4 wheat Hamburger Ns
- 4 arugulas
- chopped HeartMate 4 slices
- cucumber yogurt dill sauce
- 1 cup Kody Sushmita chopped
- 1 cup Grid
- 2 f Mc
- ¼ teaspoon
- Salt
- Fresh black juice
- 1 tbsp fresh dill chopped
- 1 tbsp vegetable Tel Kino

Instructions

- Make during saucepan quinoa, rinse in cold water, it rotates together with your hands until a dry husk is not the surface Go Also dry the quinoa as you will place the saucepan on the stovetop. Turn the heat to medium-high and dry the quinoa on the stovetop, shaking the pan regularly until you see the quinoa moving easily and the seeds occupying the pan. Add water, salt, and pepper. Bring liquid to a boil then reduce heat to medium-low. You just want to see a couple of bubbles, not a boil. Cover with the lid, leaving it sequel (or if you put a spout, just put the lid on the pot) and boil for 20 minutes. Turn off the heat and inflate the quinoa with a fork. If there is any liquid left inside the bottom of the pot, put it back on the burner for about 3 minutes. Spread the cooked quinoa on a sheet pan to cool.

- Combine space temperature quinoa during a large bowl with oats, eggs, onions, cheese, and herbs. Season with salt and pepper and mix well. Shape the mixture into 4 patties. Add a touch of water or an addition of more oatmeal to urge the mixture to be the proper consistency to make the patty.
- Spray each side of the patties generously with oil and transfer them to the basket of the air fryer in one layer (you will need to cook these burgers in a count on the dimensions of your air fryer). Air-fry, each batch at 400°F for 10 minutes, flipping more than half the burgers through the cooking time.

- While the burgers are cooking, make a cucumber curd sauce by mixing all the ingredients during a bowl.
- Build your burger on whole-wheat hamburger buns with arugula, tomato and so cucumber yogurt sauce.

Air Fried Unsaturated Veggies

Ingredients

- Vegan Stuffed 2 Large Idaho / Russet Baking Potatoes Unsaturated Veg
- 1 to 2 Tablespoons of Vegetable Oil Leave Oil to Make Free,
- 1/4 Cupcake
- 1/4 Cup Non-Dairy Milk

- 2 Tbsp Nutritional Yeast
- 1 /. 2 teaspoons salt subforum salt-free for your favorite salt-free
- 1/4 teaspoon pepper
- 1 cup chopped spinach or cabbage
- optional Topping Ingredients:
- 1/4 cup sweet vegetarian yogurt
- smoked salt and pepper
- chopped chives parsley or other favorite fresh herbs Bootie

Instructions

- Rub each potato with oil on all sides.
- Preheat your air fryer to 390 ° until your model requires it. Once it is hot, put the potato in the basket of your air fryer.
- Set the cooking time to half an hour and when it's time, flip the potatoes and cook for 30 minutes.
- Note: Depending on the dimensions of your potato, you will need to cook for 10 to 20 minutes ahead. You will know that once they are ready, you can easily pierce it with a fork.
- Let the potatoes cool enough that you can touch them without burning yourself.
- Cut each potato in half lengthwise and sieve the center of the potato periodically, leaving enough to form a thin layer of potato peel and white portion.

- Mash the scooped potatoes, veg curd, non-dairy milk, nutritional yeast, salt, and pepper until smooth.
- Stir within the chopped spinach and fill the potato shells with the mixture.
- Depending on the dimensions of your air fryer, you will be ready to cook all 4 parts at once; otherwise, you may need to cook 2 of them at once.
- Cook at 350 degrees for five minutes (or set that often as close as your air fryer).
- Serve with the topping options of your choice and enjoy!

Conclusion

Thank you for making it through to the end of Mediterranean Diet Air Fryer Cookbook, let's hope it was informative and able to provide you with all of the tools you need to achieve your goals whatever they may be.

The objective of this guide is to help you discover all the benefits and alternatives of preparing Mediterranean Diet meals to easily learn how to prepare and plan healthy and balanced meals for every day of the week and to start saving time, money, calories, and energy!

We also hope you will find the recipes we shared with you useful and enjoyable, on how to plan a balanced breakfast, lunch, and dinner quickly and easily for the whole family.

Finally, if you found this book useful in any way, a review is always appreciated!